The Good University Guide for IB Students
UK Edition 2016

The Good University Guide for IB Students
UK Edition 2016

ALEXANDER ZOUEV
ROMAN ZOUEV

ZOUEV PUBLISHING

This book is printed on acid-free paper.

Copyright © 2015 Alexander Zouev. All rights reserved.

No part of this book may be used or reproduced in any manner whatsoever without written permission, except in the case of brief quotations embodied in critical articles or reviews.

Published 2015
Printed by Lightning Source

ISBN 978-0-9934187-0-9, paperback.

Dedicated to you, the student.

TABLE OF CONTENTS

How and When to Apply	7
What to Study	8
Where to Study	11
The UCAS Form	14
List: Top Ten International Universities	18
UNIVERISTY PAGES	
Aston University	21
Bath, University of	23
Birmingham, University of	25
Bournemouth University of	27
Bristol, University of	29
Buckingham, University of	31
Cambridge, University of	33
Cardiff, University of	35
Cass Business School (City University	37
Central Lancashire, University of	39
Central Saint Martin (University of the Arts, London)	41
Durham University	43
Edinburgh, University of	45
Essex, University of	47
Exeter, University of	49
European Business School	51
Imperial College London	53
Kent, University of	55
Kings College London	57
London College of Fashion (University of the Arts, London)	59
London College of Communication	61
London School of Economics and Political Sciences	63
Loughborough, University of	65
Manchester, University of	67
Northumbria University	69
Nottingham, University of	71
Oxford, University of	73
Portsmouth, University of	75
Queen Mary, University of London	77
Reading, University of	79
Regent's Business School (Regent's College)	81
Royal Holloway, University of London	83
University College London	85
Warwick, University of	87
York, University of	89

Introduction

Congratulations on obtaining the only UK university guidebook aimed specifically at helping IB students get the higher education that they deserve. Before we get into the specifics, I would like to outline my motivation for putting this book together and why it is important for you to read it.

First and foremost, it is no secret that the International Baccalaureate program is still miles behind the A-Level program in terms of worldwide recognition and university acceptance. While the program has made leaps and bounds over the last decade, there is still a long way to go before it can overtake the A-Level program in terms of popularity and acknowledgment. The implications of this for current students are pretty immense. Almost all of the information and help (both free and non-free) is aimed at A-Level students and very UK-centric. Apart from an occasional conversion table showing IB scores alongside A-Level points and their respective UCAS tariffs, not much else is done to cater to IB students.

On the outset, this may not seem like much of a worry for most. After all, most of the information on universities is helpful regardless of where you studied or what you know. However when you start to take into account the fact that IB students tend to come from foreign places, unfamiliar with the UK education system and local customs, you start to feel that there is a gap in information.

This book aims to shed light on some of the questions that IB students will want answered before they apply to study abroad in the UK. We profile students at the top universities and ask questions such as: 'are the IB requirements fair?', 'are international students well taken care of?', 'is it hard to integrate?' and 'would you recommend this to other IB students?' Moreover, the first few sections of this book will guide you through the application process and what you can do as an

IB student to maximize your chances of getting into the best universities.

We hope that this book will spur a wider movement where universities and independent educational guides take greater notice of IB students and recognize that the rise in the popularity of the program is very real. We also hope that this information is digested properly by IB students, so that we can have even more feedback and university guides in future editions of the book.

Choosing which university to attend, or whether to go to university at all after two intense years of the International Baccalaureate program is no easy decision. This guidebook aims to help those students who have their hearts set on higher education in the United Kingdom. UK universities have grown in popularity among international students for many years and the trend has accelerated as courses become more affordable and accessible. Despite rises in visa charges and slight changes in immigration policy, enthusiasm for high education in the UK has not dimmed.

UK universities have gained reputations as cosmopolitan places that welcome international students with open arms, especially those with an IB education. Britain has become one of the world's most popular study destinations, not far behind the USA. Large number of students come from China, India, USA, Hong Kong and Singapore. Within the EU, the most popular countries to send students to the UK tend to be from France, Germany and Poland.

Whether you dream about studying in Oxford or Cambridge, or want to lose yourself in the urban grittiness of London or Manchester, the UK has endless possibilities for higher education. There are countless reasons for wanting to study in England, but least the fact that an internationally respected will be reward for all that study. You will get to widen your horizons and learn something new about yourself in the process.

International students are attracted to the UK primarily because of the worldwide reputation and recognition of the universities and qualifications, high standards of teaching and research, and the quality of life. The declining value of the pound means that the cost of studying in the UK may be higher; however this has not deterred many students. Within the UK, costs vary greatly by geographical area. London is the most expensive place to live, and accommodation costs can be relatively high in other major cities.

When deciding which university to choose, a number of factors should be taken into account. The availability, type and cost of accommodation is important. The university location and how easy it will be to get around. Also you will want to know how good the job prospects are upon graduation. This information can be found in a multitude of university guides available to purchase or in any major library.

Unlike any major university guide, what this book aims to do achieve is a complete guide to university catered for students of the IB Diploma program. Often I see IB candidates all over the world struggling to decide which universities to apply to, and how to differentiate between them. For A-Level students living in the UK, the choice is less difficult as they have been raised with a wide array of information given to them about university prospects. Most of the guides available focus primarily on A-Level requirements needed and very little attention is paid to the 'international' aspect of universities.

This book aims to fill that information void. We offer advice and application help specifically for students of the International Baccalaureate. Everything from filling out your UCAS form, to spicing up your personal statement with CAS and ToK references will be covered. Moreover, this book provides a profile of over 40 different universities in the UK – each complete with an in-depth interview of a former IB student. Questions such as 'How does the workload compare to IB workload', 'Are there special arrangements made to accommodate overseas students' and 'Do you feel you have an advantage over A-Level students' are fully answered.

We start, however, by briefly discussing some of the factors you need to start thinking about before continuing.

Where to study in the UK

The United Kingdom is made up of England, Scotland and Wales, which we often refer to as Great Britain when we take Northern Ireland into account. The vast majority of UK universities (and most of the universities covered in this guidebook) are located in England. All undergraduates from EU countries are charged the same fees as those from the part of the UK where their chosen university is to be located. This rate was £3,290 in 2011. EU students pay no tuition fees in Scotland.

Often when overseas students think of university life in the UK, they conjure up the Oxbridge (Oxford and Cambridge) image. Where there is a traditional culture, somewhat aged. In truth however, most universities are modern institutions which place as much emphasis on teaching as social activities and offer many vocational programmes. UK universities have a worldwide reputation for the quality of their teaching and research.

UK universities gained their worldwide reputation for high quality research and teaching by continuously investing heavily in superior academic staff, university infrastructure and equipment, and by complying with intense quality assurance monitoring. The main regulatory body is the Quality Assurance Agency for higher education (QAA) and it plays an important role in handling student complaints that are not resolved internally by the universities.

What subjects to study?

Traditionally, strongly vocational courses have been favoured by overseas students. Many of these are in areas such as dentistry, architecture and medicine – professional areas that may require several years longer to complete than most other degrees. Regular first degrees are awarded at the Bachelor level (BA, BSc, BEng, etc.). There are also more 'enhanced' first degrees (MEng, MChem, etc.) that take four years to complete. Some universities also offer 'foundation' degrees that take one to two years to complete, with an option to study further in order to gain a full degree.

For IB students, subject choices will be heavily dependent on what subjects are taken at Diploma Level, and what career path you intend to follow upon graduating. Keep in mind that your IB subjects already limit your choices when deciding what to study at university – for example, one should not expect to do a serious degree in medicine without taking chemistry as a subject.

How to apply

For IB students, the most common method of application is via the Universities and Colleges Admissions Service (UCAS). You will need to fill in an online UCAS application form at home, and there is plenty of advice available on how to best do this (we will cover this later). One helpful website to start looking at is UCAS's own section aimed to help overseas students [www.ucas.com/students/wheretostart/nonukstudents].

The application deadlines are very important and you should make note of them immediately. For those of you applying from within the EU, application forms must be received by 15 January for most of the courses. Oxbridge applications are different altogether (as well as some medicine and dentistry courses) and have to be delivered to UCAS by 15 October at the latest. Various art and design courses may have a later deadline of 24 March, however you should check this on your own.

If you are applying from a non-EU country, you must submit your application to UCAS between 1st September and June 30th preceding the academic year in which you plan to start studying. It is advised to apply well in advance to allow time for immigration issues and regulations, and to make travel and accommodation arrangements.

Entry regulations

The main countries that welcome international students (USA, UK, Canada, and Australia) have made serious efforts to streamline visa processes and entry requirements in order to make them more appealing. As of September 2012, all students wishing to enter the UK to study are required to obtain entry clearance before arrival. Exceptions include British nationals living abroad and non-visa national short-term students. Further details of the latest rules and regulations can be found at the following website:
www.ukba.homeoffice.gov.uk/studyingintheuk

How and When to Apply

You must ensure that you send your application in well before the deadline, especially if you want to study at one of the top universities in the UK. Any application made to a UK university will be processed by UCAS – and you can find more specific information at the UCAS website or from your school's course coordinator.

Non-EU students can submit an application to UCAS between 1st September and June 30rd in the year preceding the academic year when they hope to start their studies. Please note however that most students apply much in advance to ensure that places are still available and allow time to make travel, immigration and accommodation arrangements.

International students from within an EU country must submit their application form to UCAS by 15th January or else they are treated as late applicants. Oxford and Cambridge set earlier dates, as do courses that offer medicine and design. You must check the deadlines of your interested courses in advance to make sure you do not miss anything.

Fees will differ for international students. Normally those that are residents outside the EU will have to pay near-full-cost tuition fees for UK universities. Moreover, these students will not be eligible for the grants and scholarships available to UK and EU students. Students from within the EU will pay the same fees as UK students. International students from outside the EU can seek some sort of financial support from their home countries (the vast majority of grants are for post-graduate study, however there are some circumstances which would allow undergraduates to gain financial support).

What to Study?

Most people start to look for university places start by choosing a subject and course, rather than a university. If you take a degree, then you should be prepared to be fully immersed in your subject for at least three years. It has to be one you will enjoy and can master – not to mention, one that you are qualified to study. Many economics degrees require maths, for example, while some medical schools demand chemistry or biology. The UCAS website contains course profiles, including entrance requirements, which is a good starting point, while universities own sites contain more detailed information.

The official yardstick by which your IB result will be judged is the UCAS tariff which gives a score for each point total received. There has been some controversy in recent years about how the points are worked out and the discrepancies between A-Levels and the IB program. Top scores in the new vocational diplomas in A-Levels, for example will attract more points than a full set of A grades at A level, while the most successful IB students already earn considerably more points. If this process continues it is likely that more of the leading universities will abandon the tariff as some have done already.

Choosing your subject at university is not always as straightforward as it sounds. Your IB subjects may have chosen themselves, but the range of subjects across the whole university system is vast. Even subjects that you have studied at school may be quite different at degree level – some academic economists actually prefer their undergraduates not to have taken IB economics because they approach the subject so differently. Indeed, this was the case for when I studied economics at Oxford. Another scenario is that students are disappointed because they appear to be going over old ground when they continue with a subject that they enjoyed at school. Universities now publish quite detailed syllabuses, and you should go through these very carefully.

If you are not sure whether you will be suited to a particular subject, you can take an online aptitude test through the UCAS website. The 'What to study' section gives you access to the Stamford Test, which uses an online questionnaire to match your interests and strengths to possible courses and careers.

You may find that more than one subject appeals to you, in which case you could consider Joint Honours – degrees that combine two subjects – or even Combined Honours, which will cover several related subjects. Such courses obviously allow you to extent the scope of your studies but they should be approached with caution. Even if the number of credits suggests a similar workload to Single Honours, covering more than one subject inevitably involves extra reading and often more essays or project work. The advantages are quite obvious. Many students choose a 'dual' degree to add a vocational element and make themselves more employable – business studies with languages or engineering for example, or media studies with English. Others want to take their studies in a particular direction, perhaps by combining history with politics, or statistics with maths. Some simply want to add a completely unrelated interest to their main subject such as archaeology and event management.

Personally, however, I feel that your university course choice needs to be a combination of a few factors but most importantly you need to have a somewhat clear picture of what you intend to do with your degree. It is not wise to have a career mapped out as an investment banker and for that reason alone try to get into an economics course at a top university. You should have some passion and interest in the course that you wish to study. At the same time, if you wish to become a dentist or something very specific, taking a course in design or art will do you no good.

For me, the choice to study economics was a rather simple one. I enjoyed maths a lot throughout highschool, and my father put a certain emphasis on doing well in both mathematics and economics because, in his words, 'it will be important for your future, regardless of what career you choose'. Although that may not be necessarily true, I did have a feeling I would end up an investment banker or working somewhere within the realms of finance or consulting. Also, given the fact that my brother had just graduated with a degree in Economics and Management from Oxford and had only good things to say, I was left with little choice but to follow in his footsteps.

You should certainly devote a significant portion of time prior to filling out your UCAS form to researching the specifics of various courses. And when I say specifics, I mean specifics. Start by browsing the websites and see if there are any timetables or course-specific materials available to the public. If not, email the departments and express your interest in applying and finding out more information. Last but not least, we live in such an interconnected world where you can find alumni from specific courses with the click of a button. Utilize Facebook and websites like studentroom.co.uk to find graduates and ask them any questions you may have.

The times are constantly changing, and whereas a few years ago a degree in 'business and management' may have been seen as the must-have diploma, many would argue that this is no longer the case. Perhaps we have reached a point where there are 'too many' business degrees available and not enough traditional and vocational applicants. I would not be surprised to see a turnaround and more students applying to become doctors or lawyers in the next few decades. Although you are only in your late teens, you should have some idea already of what you wish to become – and this should help guide your university course choice.

Where to Study?

Once you have decided what to study, there are still several factors that might influence your choice of university or college. Obviously, you need to have a reasonable chance of getting in, you may want reassurance about the university's reputation, and its location will probably also be important to you. The surveys conducted in this book aim to address all of those factors, especially from a foreigner's perspective. One top of that, most applicants have views about the type of institution they are looking for – big or small, old or new, urban or rural, specialist or comprehensive. You may surprise yourself by choosing somewhere that does not conform to your initial criteria but working through your preferences is another way of narrowing down your options.

One of the more obvious starting points when thinking about where to study is location. Most degrees in Scotland take four years, rather than the UK norm of three. Also students normally pay little to no fees in Scotland, while those from the rest of the UK do. Nevertheless, Edinburgh and St Andrews remain particularly popular with international students.

A growing number of international students tend to look at the ease of traveling home from their university location. For those coming from Europe, London is a popular choice in this department because of the Eurostar services from King's Cross and the four main city airports – City, Heathrow, Gatwick and Stansted. You should get a rough idea of the traveling required to get home during the term breaks, or even if you wanted to go home for a long weekend.

The most popular universities in terms of total applications are usually all in the big cities – generally with other major centres of population within a two-hour traveling window. For those looking for the best nightclubs, sporting events, shopping or a wide array of culture – in other words, most young people, and especially those who study in international schools close to city centres already – city universities are a magnet. The big universities also, by definition, offer the widest range of subjects, although that does not mean that they necessarily have the particular course that is right for you. Nor does it mean that you will actually use the array of nightlife and shopping that looks so alluring in the prospectus, either because you cannot afford to, because student life is too focused on the university, or even because you are too busy working.

City universities are the right choice for many young people, but it is worth bearing in mind that the National Student Survey shows that the highest satisfaction levels tend to be at smaller universities, often those with their own self-contained campuses. It seems that students identify more closely with institutions where there is a close-knit community and the social life is based around the students' union rather than the local nightclubs.

Few UK universities are in genuinely rural locations, but some – particularly among the newly promoted – are in relatively small towns. The only way to be certain of a university is to visit the university yourself. Schools often hold open days and these should certainly not be ignored. The full calendar of events is available at www.opendays.com and on universities' own websites. Bear in mind, if you only attend one or two that the event has to be badly mismanaged for a university not to seem an exciting place to someone who spends his or her days at college. Try to get a flavour of several institutions before you make your choice.

The Oxford Study Courses (OSC) company runs a University Tour program which attracts IB students. They provide private tours of at least 12 different universities and colleges, as well as giving seminars and information sessions. Guidance and advice is available from experienced careers counsellors accompanying the tours and you get a chance to talk to admission officers and understand the differences in what each university offers. If you have the time and the finances available, I strongly recommend this tour – especially to those who know very little about UK universities in general.

Again, I stress the importance of the resources at your disposal when it comes to choosing where to study – both free and not. This book should only be your starting block when it comes to doing the necessary research. Our aim is to share with you what a typical IB student feels about their university and well they fit in. By all means, please do consult the other big university guidebooks as they give a more detailed profile of universities (albeit from a UK-centric perspective), as well as providing rankings and other useful information.

The UCAS Form

When it finally comes time to making your final university choice, you will not be making one choice but five (four if you are applying for medicine, dentistry or veterinary science). Tens of thousands of students each year eventually go to a university that did not start out as their first choice either because they did not get the right offer or because they changed their mind along the way. UCAS rules are such that applicants do not list universities in order of preference anyway – indeed; universities are not allowed to know where else you have applied. Therefore it is important that you do not pin all of your hopes on one course. Take just as much care choosing the other universities on your list.

This section of the book will not guide you step by step on how to fill in your UCAS application. This information is made very clear on the UCAS website, and additional help can be found in numerous forum posts on www.thestudentroom.co.uk. I do wish to address three aspects of the UCAS application process that are almost unique to IB students, and therefore should be given extra attention: predicted grades, recommendations and the personal statement.

Those of you who have read my book on succeeding in the IB program, *I Think Therefore IB*, will remember how much I stressed the importance of grade predictions. Unlike the A-Level program, where students already have what are known as A2s (first year exams) as a sort of predictor of final results, there is no such mid-way assessment in the IB. Due to this, IB students applying via UCAS do not fill in a predicted grades section. Your teachers however, do submit something very similar.

Predicted grades are a tricky obstacle for any IB student. Nine times out of ten, students will feel that they are being under-predicted. Many schools refuse to disclose the predictions to students because they anticipate a large angry group of kids mobbing them with protests after school hours. Nonetheless, predicted grades are the golden ticket when it comes to university offers. If your predicted grades are below the usual entry standards, the chances of you receiving an offer from a UK university are slim to none.

Here is my simple advice when it comes to maximizing your chances of getting the best predicted grades: negotiation. The matter of the fact is that teachers often look at things like homework grades, test results and class participation as an indicator of how well you will do in the final IB examinations. Although some of those things may play a small role, the truth is that the best predictors of your final results are: internal assessments (coursework that counts towards your final grade), how well you take IB examinations, how well you prepared in the few months before examinations, and a small element of random luck. Luck and exam revision aside, the other two components are fairly easy to analyse.

If your teachers insist on looking at test scores and random homework assignments as a way to judge your future success in the final exams, you need to persuade them that your high-scoring courseworks (which account for 20-40% of final subject grades in most subjects) and your ability to study past-paper questions and handle mock exams are both a far better indicator of how well you will do. I understand that this is easier said than done, but I do remember spending a good week or so visiting various teachers after-hours to ensure them that despite my so-so homework grades or sometimes uninspired class participation, I will score highly on my diploma because I know what counts and I know how to play the IB system. Those of you who have read my IB help book will know exactly what I am talking about.

Closely related to the topic of predicted grades, another factor that will set your application apart from the rest is the reference written by your teacher. It is absolutely imperative that the person who you choose to write your reference is someone who is not only highly literate, but more importantly can fill the reference full of praise and admiration. Obviously, the person writing your reference should be closely related to the subject you intend to study at university. There are minor exceptions to this. For example, when I was applying to study economics, my economics teacher at school did not necessarily dislike me, however I did feel that they would not put all of their efforts into writing a stand-out reference and perhaps it would not be as elegantly written. Instead, I sought the help of my geography teacher (who happened to hold a PhD from LSE, and had previously taught economics and business at a high school level). The teacher in question clearly saw a lot of potential in me, so I asked for help and got a wonderfully written reference in return. Whoever you seek for this task, make sure they are not going to write a generic reference but instead something personal and something that will make you stand out.

Too many students do not consider the importance of the reference. Keep in mind that top universities want to know that you are a person who is passionate about their studies and can cope well with a university workload. They will trust the words of your teachers/superiors more than anything else. You must ensure that you seek out the best possible candidate to write your reference and you must ensure that they do the best that they can.

Last but not least is the personal statement that you must write and submit in your UCAS application. Again, I want to refrain from going into too much detail about what makes a great personal statement – the UCAS guide and the online student forums are filled with excellent tips and advice. What I want to focus on is how you, the IB student, will be able to get the maximum out of your diploma status.

Put yourself into the shoes of a university admissions officer. You must go through thousands of personal statements, the vast majority of which come from A-level students in both private, but mainly public schools in the UK. They will write about how they nearly became head boy/girl and how they really enjoyed their participation in the Duke of Edinburgh award (if neither of these things made sense to you, don't worry – they are terms that only a typical British student would normally understand). The point I am trying to make is that the vast majority of students applying through the British school system have very little that will differentiate themselves amongst the other candidates. They will talk about their GCSE's and how they are coping with their A-Levels and how they play football for their local team. All of this is fine, but it gets boring and repetitive. Admissions officers are looking for something with added spice.

Here is where the IB Diploma program comes into play. You need to use the notion that the IB program is not as well-known as the A-levels to your advantage. Write about how your Extended Essay gave you a good sense of what a university level paper requires. Explain how CAS enabled you to participate in the community and make a difference. Talk about ToK, and lab reports, and learning a foreign language. Those of you studying in International Schools, make sure to play the 'culture card'. Admission officers eat that stuff up. Talk about how you have friends from all over the world, and how you have learnt about new cultures and religions and this has made you see the world in a different light. Do you get the point?

You need to realise that your application is unique in the sense that you are studying in an environment that is vastly different from most other applicants. The IB Diploma program is difficult and strenuous, but also highly respectable and rewarding. You need to convey these messages across your personal statement, and then add something extra to make yourself stand out from other IB applicants.

Top 10 International Universities

Overseas students are not a rarity in the UK. Below is a list of the top ten universities with the most international students, including EU students from outside the UK.

1. University of Buckingham

2. LSE

3. Royal Academy of Music

4. University of Essex

5. SOAS

6. Royal College of Music

7. University of Warwick

8. Imperial College, London

9. Middlesex University

10. London Metropolitan University

Source: http://www.push.co.uk

Useful Links

- Education UK website [www.educationuk.org]

- UK Council for International student Affairs [www.ukcisa.org.uk]

- The British Council [www.britishcouncil.org.uk]
The Government-backed website promoting UK education and culture to our foreign friends. Useful information about how the UK higher education system works for international students, how to apply and potential sources of funding.

- Education UK [www.educationuk.org]
Information about studying in the UK from the British Council

- UKCOSA (The Council for International Education) [www.ukcosa.org.uk]
Advice for anyone from abroad thinking of studying in the UK and for anyone in the UK thinking of studying abroad. Really helpful.

-Univisits [www.univisits.com]
Univisits lays on tours of universities in the UK and Ireland. There are special tour packages or they can tailor one to suit your needs - this includes travel, accommodation and food.

University Profiles

Aston University
Tel. +441212043000; www.aston.ac.uk

Student Name:
Milena Dimitrova

IB World School:
Nørre Gymnasium (Copenhagen)

Nationality:
Bulgarian

What course do you currently study?
BSc Business and International Relations, Third Year

University offer:
32

How does your workload at university compare to the IB Diploma?
It is about the same. The main difference is that at university students are responsible for managing their own workloads, which makes it more difficult and challenging.

Would you say you have an advantage over A-Level students in your studies? How?

IB courses are more similar than A-levels to the ones at university. IB examinations and internal assessment project excellently prepare students for university. In my particular case, IB provided an excellent background to the material, which was largely covered during the first year at university.

Is there any element of the IB that you have found particularly useful in your university studies?

The Extended Essay is quite useful, especially for people who are pursuing a degree in Politics/History/International Relations. These subjects require students to write a lot of essays, which need to be in a similar format. The Extended Essay gives students a taste of what university essay-writing will be like. In addition, the IB offers a lot of flexibility so students can specialise in the subjects that they find particularly interesting.

Did you find your personal requirements fair? Do you feel the offer under/overrated the IB system?

I think they were fair. In fact, I believe the IB was highly valued by my university and I found the requirements lower compared to A-levels.

How does the social life compare to the one you had at school?

University offers a better social life than school. There are many more opportunities to socialise and meet a broad range of people if compared to school. In addition, the fact that most people live on campus means everybody is close and it is much easier to organise events or simply hang out in one of the many facilities campus offers. Aston has many societies that cover a very broad range of interests/sports/hobbies - there is anything from the Trading and Investment Society, to Model United Nations and a Travelling Society. Campus has excellent sports facilities including a football pitch, swimming pool and two sports halls.

Are there special efforts made to accommodate international students?

Aston has a very high percentage of international students from around the world and it makes sure they are all looked after well. There are many events specifically targeted at international students, such as cultural fairs, short trips around the UK, drop-in sessions. There is an information hub as well, which provides information regarding visas, accommodation opportunities, university life, bursaries and anything else international students might have queries about.

Are there many former IB students? Do you socialize with them?

A lot of the students from other European countries are former IB students. Many of my friends are as well. Having studied the IB proved to be an excellent conversation starter especially in the first few weeks at university.

Would you recommend your university to prospective IB students?

I would recommend the university because it provides good quality education, is located in a big city and encourages all students to take a year out and do either a work or a study placement. However, although Aston provides a lot of support for international students, events seem to be designed predominantly with students from outside of Europe in mind. Also, most modules are not very interactive and I feel that, to certain extent, creativity and independent thinking are not encouraged to the same extent as in the IB.

Further Statistics and Information

Students		Accommodation	
Undergraduates:	7,235	University-provided places:	2,300
Postgraduates:	1,855	Percentage catered:	0%
Overseas students:	20.1%	Self-catered costs (per week):	£68-£120
Applications per place:	6.2		
From state-sector schools:	91.3%	**Undergraduate Fees**	
From working-class homes:	37.1%	Fees for UK/EU students:	£3,290
		International Student fees:	£10,700 - £12,250

University of Bath

Tel. +441225 383012; www.bath.ac.uk

Student Name:
Jim Ashford

IB World School:
ACS Hillingdon (London)

Nationality:
American

What course do you currently study?
Economics, Third Year

University offer:
36 points

How does your workload at university compare to the IB Diploma?

The workload in terms of quantity is certainly less than it was in IB. In terms of depth and understanding however, the degree that I am doing does involve a lot of difficult concepts that are very different from IB Economics. I do find that I have more free time at university than I did during the two years of IB

Would you say you have an advantage over A-Level students in your studies? How?

Most definitely. I find that the A-Level students have had far less experience with demanding deadlines and are not accustomed to juggling many tasks at once and prioritising – certainly not as much as the IB students. Also, the fact that each and every one of us had to keep literature, math, and a science during our last two years of high school means the IB students are much better-rounded than an A-level student who stuck to very similar subjects.

Is there any element of the IB that you have found particularly useful in your university studies?

Yes, HL Economics and HL Mathematics proved to be invaluable for my course in particular. In fact the whole 'investigative thinker' mind-set that the IB encourages helped me greatly at university. Also, in terms of essay writing, the experience I gained when writing the EE was very helpful. I certainly feel that I am more organised and have a better sense of time-management than my fellow A-level peers. Also, coping with stress and meeting deadlines is not much of an issue

Did you find your personal requirements fair? Do you feel the offer under/overrated the IB system?

It is difficult to say. On the one hand, a direct comparison to the A-Level requirements would suggest that those taking the IB program have quite a bit more to do. On the whole however, I feel that the requirements were not too bad given the quality of education I got in return.

How does the social life compare to the one you had at school?

The social life is pretty comparable – a high number of students were educated at independent schools. Sometimes the campus can be a bit too quite on weekends, but Bristol city is located just a few minutes away for a livelier nightlife.

Are there special efforts made to accommodate international students?

There is a good percentage of foreign kids, and they tend to get along really well with one another. The students' union is pretty active, and they do make efforts to add a bit of an 'international' vibe to some of their events. Your best bet to meet a variety of nationalities is to join a sports team – something that Bath excels at.

Are there many former IB students? Do you socialize with them?

There are, however besides the occasional joke about how difficult the IB was, I would not say that the IB kids conglomerate together specifically. It's sometimes nice to reminisce about the sleepless nights writing the EE with another IB student; however most of my friends now are from a non-IB background.

Would you recommend your university to prospective IB students?

Certainly! The University of Bath is great for a wide variety of degrees. Everybody that attends Bath has absolutely no regrets about their time spent here. I suggest that prospective students take a weekend and come to an open day to see how great Bath really is.

Further Statistics and Information

Students		Accommodation	
Undergraduates:	8.890	University-provided places:	3,354
Postgraduates:	1,545	Percentage catered:	0%
Overseas students:	21.6%	Self-catered costs (per week):	£85 - £130
Applications per place:	6.8		
From state-sector schools:	76.8%	**Undergraduate Fees**	
From working-class homes:	19.0%	Fees for UK/EU students:	£3,290
		International Student fees:	£11,000 - £14,000

University of Birmingham
Tel. +441214158900; www.bham.ac.uk

Student Name:
Rupert Turner

IB World School:
United Nations International School, Hanoi

Nationality:
Chilean

What course do you currently study?
Final year; International Relations with Spanish

University offer:
33

How does your workload at university compare to the IB Diploma?

While the work load on a daily basis is less, the intensity and demands of the work load are higher. Also what must be observed is that more self-instilled discipline is needed due to a lack of guidance compared with what you receive at school.

Would you say you have an advantage over A-Level students in your studies? How?

I would like to think I do. Not only down to the wide range of material covered by the IB but also the fact that my background of international schooling has led me to have a perspective on things that is not often considered by A-level/UK students.

Is there any element of the IB that you have found particularly useful in your university studies?

I took history higher level which required high volumes of essay writing that I personally believe was essential to my success at University. Learning how to properly use sources and citations was also a crucial aspect of the IB program.

Did you find your personal requirements fair? Do you feel the offer under/overrated the IB system?

I thought it was very fair. While it challenged me I appreciated the challenge. I do feel however that the IB is in danger of been ignored by UK universities, as they would rather seek the money provided to them by foreign students (non-EU), most who I do not believe do the IB take up the international quotas of universities.

How does the social life compare to the one you had at school?

Social life is as good. It is a completely different scenario from what it was at school, it offers a whole new cultural insight that one is often not aware of. Student facilities on campus are on par with the best in the country. The campus is less than three miles from Birmingham centre, and the area has plenty of shops, pubs and restaurants of its own. We have our own nightclub among the facilities so some students do not even stray that far out.

Are there special efforts made to accommodate international students?

Indeed there are, if you want to be part of the international community at university it is more than easy. Birmingham as a city is also very welcoming to diverse and international cultures. It regularly lists among the top universities in the nightlife rankings.

Are there many former IB students? Do you socialize with them?

Not that I know of. I am sure there are but it's not something that I have taken note of.

Would you recommend your university to prospective IB students?

There are aspects of it I would, such as a vast international society in which IB students thrive, but also at times there is a frustration with a lack of understanding of perspectives from both the institutions and lecturers. On the whole, the university is growing in both stature and reputation so prospective IB students can take note.

Further Statistics and Information

Students		Accommodation	
Undergraduates:	**16,740**	University-provided places:	4,267
Postgraduates:	**5,685**	Percentage catered:	42%
Overseas students:	**9.8%**	Self-catered costs (per week):	£77–£160
Applications per place:	**7.1**		
From state-sector schools:	**81.0%**	**Undergraduate Fees**	
From working-class homes:	**23.3%**	Fees for UK/EU students:	£3,290
		International Student fees:	£10,800–£14,000

Bournemouth University

Tel. +441202961961; www.bournemouth.ac.uk

Student Name:
Stephan Moehrke

IB World School:
International School of Hamburg

Nationality:
South African

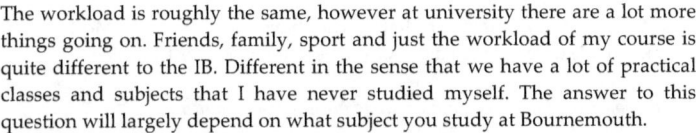

What course do you currently study?
First year, Physiotherapy

University offer:
29 points

How does your workload at university compare to the IB Diploma?

The workload is roughly the same, however at university there are a lot more things going on. Friends, family, sport and just the workload of my course is quite different to the IB. Different in the sense that we have a lot of practical classes and subjects that I have never studied myself. The answer to this question will largely depend on what subject you study at Bournemouth.

Would you say you have an advantage over A-Level students in your studies? How?

I wouldn't say so, because students in A Levels are only required as far as I know to take 3 subjects minimum, whereas in the IB one has to take maths, an A1 language, a science and a second language. It is also required to take a human science, e.g. geography, economics, history etc. Students in A-Levels seem to have a more in depth knowledge in biology compared to a student who studied biology at an IB level. This is simply because the student in A-levels has to solely focus on his/her 3 subjects and an IB student on 6 official subjects and then Extended Essay, Theory of Knowledge. The IB is a work overload system with detail but in my opinion not as much as A-level detail.

Is there any element of the IB that you have found particularly useful in your university studies?

So far, not really. Obviously the time management skills and the ability to cope under stress and with deadlines looming is something that any IB student can relate to.

Did you find your personal requirements fair? Do you feel the offer under/overrated the IB system?

My personal requirements were very fair. It did not overrate nor underrate the IB system. It seemed fair and completely worth it.

How does the social life compare to the one you had at school?

Social life very similar however much cheaper if you are used to previously living in a large city. I have friends all over the place and there is not a day that goes by without me seeing someone I know in Bournemouth. The seaside location is ideal for those who want to get away from the city. The area has plenty to offer students during the summer season. The student's union Old Fire Station bar is a favourite among nightlife options.

Are there special efforts made to accommodate international students?

Yes there is, however I am not part of any international student groups. International students do make up a small minority however this has never been a problem. There is however a large amount of interesting societies to keep students occupied.

Are there many former IB students? Do you socialize with them?

No, there are not many students who have done the IB. Most of the international students you come across are usually former IB students.

Would you recommend your university to prospective IB students?

Yes I would recommend my university to do so, because generally IB students are very hard working and mostly manage with the constant threat that comes with the next work load. IB students generally come from a more international background which may be useful in certain professions.(to have another ethnic point of view) The IB is also a very hard two year system which challenges every individual who takes it. Pass or fail the IB a student must be admired for being able to complete such a hard 2 years.

Further Statistics and Information

Students		Accommodation	
Undergraduates:	11,565	University-provided places:	2,910
Postgraduates:	1,305	Percentage catered:	0%
Overseas students:	6.0%	Self-catered costs (per week):	£78-£95
Applications per place:	4.9		
From state-sector schools:	95.2%	**Undergraduate Fees**	
From working-class homes:	31.0%	Fees for UK/EU students:	£3,290
		International Student fees:	£9,000 - £14,000

University of Bristol

Tel. +441179289000; www.bristol.ac.uk

Student Name:
Laura Adcroft

IB World School:
Antwerp International School

Nationality:
American

What course do you currently study?
Graduated, MBChB; Medicine and Surgery

University offer:
39 points

How does your workload at university compare to the IB Diploma?

First year medicine was similar workload and intermittently I needed to work as hard, however IB was more consistent hard work and was probably the most demanding thing I've ever needed to do academically.

Would you say you have an advantage over A-Level students in your studies? How?

Better able to balance my workload and better at not stressing over cumulative exams. I did not feel I struggled with the science either compared to my peers despite the fact that A-levels are supposedly more in depth but less breadth – something I did not find to be true. I feel IB Biology and Chemistry adequately prepared me for a top medicine degree.

Is there any element of the IB that you have found particularly useful in your university studies?

Extended essay was good - prepared me for longer essay writing such as dissertations and as I did mine in Biology it prepared me for lab based assignments and write-ups at university. The whole IB framework of having labs and essays assessed using markschemes surprisingly makes you much more organised when having to carry out labs at university.

Did you find your personal requirements fair? Do you feel the offer under/overrated the IB system?

1st time around when applying I was given offers much too difficult however I feel that with the more recent higher rating of UCAS point for IB subjects and IGCSEs the balance has shifted and it is a more fair system. My offers were equivalent to approximately 5 A's at A level for some universities offering UK A level students much lower offers. However this time around IB appeared to be more highly valued

How does the social life compare to the one you had at school?

Similar, but more time to socialize. The city is one of the most attractive in Britain, as well as possessing a vibrant youth culture. In terms of job opportunities to students and graduates, it is very prosperous. The current student's union is less of a social centre than in some universities, partly because of the competition from the nightclubs. Students tend to really enjoy life in Bristol; however the high cost of living can be a drawback. The winter months can be a bit too sedative, and some students have raised the issue of crime and security as a concern (although personally I don't think this is a problem specific to Bristol).

Are there special efforts made to accommodate international students?

I imagine so but I've never got involved though. The amount of foreign students will vary greatly subject to subject. There is a very impressive university sports complex for any serious athletes.

Are there many former IB students? Do you socialize with them?

There are a few and it's always exciting to meet another one but it's not something I actively seek out.

Would you recommend your university to prospective IB students?

Absolutely. It is a fantastic university located in the best part of Bristol with great access to the city centre. I have even chosen to stay and work here now that my degree is finished. I highly recommend it.

Further Statistics and Information

Students		Accommodation	
Undergraduates:	12,465	University-provided places:	3,827
Postgraduates:	4,050	Percentage catered:	47%
Overseas students:	10.3%	Self-catered costs (per week):	£58-£130
Applications per place:	11.7		
From state-sector schools:	60.0%	**Undergraduate Fees**	
From working-class homes:	14.2%	Fees for UK/EU students:	£3,290
		International Student fees:	£11,900-£14,500

University of Buckingham
Tel. +441280 814080; www.buckingham.ac.uk

Student Name:
Githinji Karinge

IB World School:
The International School of Brussels

Nationality:
Nigerian

What course do you currently study?
Final Year; BSc Business and Management with French and Spanish

University offer:
30

How does your workload at university compare to the IB Diploma?

Workload at university is very much less stressful compared to that of the IB Diploma. The IB Diploma workload felt heavier seeing as we had less time to do it.

Would you say you have an advantage over A-Level students in your studies? How?

Yes; because everyone who did the IB Diploma feels that they did five times more work and went through more stress than A-level students to get to the same place. A-level students had half the amount of courses that IB Diploma students had along with fewer requirements and obstacles to achieve.

Is there any element of the IB that you have found particularly useful in your university studies?

IB Math Higher Level made Quantitative Methods very simple to understand. Otherwise, I cannot think of anything else that may have been useful. High school courses versus University courses are very different. I just hope experience with my Extended Essay will help me during my future dissertation or thesis.

Did you find your personal requirements fair? Do you feel the offer under/overrated the IB system?

I thought my personal requirements were fair relative to everyone who did the IB but in comparison to other students who did A-levels or even SATs (in the case of the US), I feel each offer underrated the IB system.

How does the social life compare to the one you had at school?

Social life is better at university than at school. Living independently (without your parents) on campus or near campus changes the whole dynamic of your social life. There is more freedom to do what we want without having to ask for permission from parents and we are generally surrounded by students at all times whereas at school, I would go home to my family every evening. The social scene is sometimes too quiet, given the size of the university and the workload, especially on the weekends. There is a university cinema and the town is pretty with a good selection of pubs and restaurants. Milton Keynes and Oxford are both nearby, although Buckingham does not have a rail station so the bus service is required.

Are there special efforts made to accommodate international students?

Yes there are various societies for international students to associate with and overseas representatives present along with special welcome packages to facilitate the early days in a new environment.

Are there many former IB students? Do you socialize with them?

I am sure there are but that has never been a criteria to start new friendships or simply mix. In my university, not too many people talk about their respective High School diplomas.

Would you recommend your university to prospective IB students?

Yes; because in any case, the IB Diploma is designed to facilitate any future University endeavours. It is a small yet very friendly university. Campus facilities are constantly improving and student numbers are also increasing. Class sizes are very small so this benefits those who are looking to get almost a one-to-one tuition.

Further Statistics and Information

Students		Accommodation	
Undergraduates:	695	University-provided places:	465
Postgraduates:	285	Percentage catered:	0%
Overseas students:	61.5%	Self-catered costs (per week):	£95
Applications per place:	0		
From state-sector schools:	86.8%	**Undergraduate Fees**	
From working-class homes:	N/A	Fees for UK/EU students:	£8,640
		International Student fees:	£19,677

University of Cambridge

Tel. +441223 33308; www.cam.ac.uk

Student Name:
Moxi Shah

IB World School:
British School of Brussels

Nationality:
Indian

What course do you currently study?
First year Theology and Religious Studies

University offer:
40 points with 776 at HL

How does your workload at university compare to the IB Diploma?

Exponentially more work at university! This is not something that is surprising for a place like Cambridge, however I would say that workload varies greatly subject to subject and sometimes even college to college. Admittedly, the actual amount of class-time (tutorials, not including lectures) most students have in a week will not exceed a few hours, but this is both a burden and a gift as it means that there is a lot of individual self-study time.

Would you say you have an advantage over A-Level students in your studies? How?

Yes in the sense that had a wider range of subjects. No, in the sense that the A-level kids had better depth in their chosen subjects. Again, this will largely depend on what course you are studying. For something like mathematics, I would imagine someone who took 3 different A-levels focusing on solely mathematics would be at an advantage over somebody who took HL Mathematics but still had to worry about 5 other subjects.

Is there any element of the IB that you have found particularly useful in your university studies?

TOK essay because Theology is almost TOK to the next level. Internal assessments because the word limit for those essays is the norm now. Students at Oxbridge are expected to write around 2,000 words on average every week – however this is something that becomes almost second nature after a few weeks. I did feel however that my ability to do research and lengthy writing was much better than the student who took A-levels.

Did you find your personal requirements fair? Do you feel the offer under/overrated the IB system?

It's no surprise that universities in general underrate the IB system but the offer was fair for the University of Cambridge. They need to challenge their prospective students. However, that being said, I think students studying the IB should feel confident because you are not directly competing with A-level students and slowly universities are starting to realise that a 40+ at IB is nowhere near 3 A's at A-level. Cambridge requests sample work and invites students for interviews so candidates are not solely competing on grades.

How does the social life compare to the one you had at school?
More lively, more time to meet people, more opportunities to make friends. Admittedly, there are only a handful of 'clubs', however the events organised by societies can sometimes turn out more attractive than the usual nightlife.

Are there special efforts made to accommodate international students?

Loads of societies for different countries are a great help. Each college has an 'overseas representative' who ensures that overseas students get all of the help they can with regards to adjusting to brutish culture, storage issues, and transportation help.

Are there many former IB students? Do you socialize with them?

Have not really met too many, it seems like almost everyone at my college at least is a former A-level student or studied a lesser known program abroad. Cambridge is a massive university though, so I'm sure this will vary college to college.

Would you recommend your university to prospective IB students?

Of course, it has amazing student help facilities, financial help is always available. The college system works well in terms of finding your group of friends. The supervisions allow one on one interaction with people trained to be one of the best in the field worldwide.

Further Statistics and Information

Students		Accommodation	
Undergraduates:	11,910	University-provided places:	(college specific)
Postgraduates:	5,615	Percentage catered:	N/A
Overseas students:	13.2%	Self-catered costs (per week):	N/A
Applications per place:	4.6		
From state-sector schools:	59.3%	**Undergraduate Fees**	
From working-class homes:	12.6%	Fees for UK/EU students:	£3,290
		International Student fees:	£10,752-14,100

University of Cardiff
Tel. +442920874455; www.cardiff.ac.uk

Student Name:
Laura Knoll

IB World School:
Antwerp International School

Nationality:
British

What course do you currently study?
Sociology and Criminology

University offer:
34

How does your workload at university compare to the IB Diploma?

In university you are much more independent, both for coursework and exams. As the markers only see your student number, it is completely unbiased unlike the IB where you had a personal relationship with each teacher, even though it was externally graded. In the IB the extended essay (4000 words) seemed like an infinite amount of work, but in university my coursework tends to be between 3500-5000 words, and my course usually requires me to write at least 3 of these essays each semester, totalling to six 3500-5000 essays a year, on top of exams. Even though the workload is a lot greater, it doesn't feel like there is such a big difference between that and the work we had to do during the IB. The main reason for this is that there is a ridiculous amount of pressure on you during the course of the IB as it is the 2 year final program to complete, whereas I expected this great amount of work in university.

Would you say you have an advantage over A-Level students in your studies? How?

I do feel like I have an advantage over A-level students as the IB is considered a more 'valuable' and 'difficult' diploma to obtain. For example, we have 6 subjects and TOK, extended essay and CAS. If I'm not mistaken, the A-levels are only 3 subjects. I know that universities regard IB diploma's as more desirable, which I feel automatically gives me an edge over A-level students.

Is there any element of the IB that you have found particularly useful in your university studies?

Certainly the Extended Essay and Theory of Knowledge have been helpful in my course. Also in general I feel that the IB has made me a much more 'well-rounded' student.

Did you find your personal requirements fair? Do you feel the offer under/overrated the IB system?

For a top UK university, which Cardiff University is, I feel like my requirement of 34 points is perfectly acceptable. It is an obtainable goal for most bright individuals to reach, but at the same time does differentiate between students' abilities.

How does the social life compare to the one you had at school?

Once again, at university you are confronted with exceptional freedom, including in your social life. It is a much bigger pool of students, and combining studies with an active social life is something most UK university students can do successfully. I would say that my social life is much greater in university than it was during the IB, but perhaps that has to do with age too.

Are there special efforts made to accommodate international students?

I know that Cardiff University offers many different societies for international students eg. Dutch society, Asian society, American society. I haven't taken part in the international orientated societies, as I feel that when you live and study in another country, you should try and adapt and integrate as well as you can.

Are there many former IB students? Do you socialize with them?

I have only met about 2 or 3 other people that have done the IB, and they all went to international schools as well. It can be fun to compare grades and talk about the experience, but I wouldn't say I socialize with them more than non-IB students. It just so happened that some of the people I met and became friends with had also done the IB.

Would you recommend your university to prospective IB students?

I would definitely recommend Cardiff University. It is one of the top schools in the UK, but more than that, Cardiff is an incredible city to live and study in, and there are so many opportunities for you to take advantage of. There is truly something for everyone, and the city of Cardiff itself is buzzing. It really is the perfect place to experience university life.

Further Statistics and Information

Students		Accommodation	
Undergraduates:	16,245	University-provided places:	5,549
Postgraduates:	3,805	Percentage catered:	5%
Overseas students:	8.2%	Self-catered costs (per week):	£64-£88
Applications per place:	6.3		
From state-sector schools:	85.2%	**Undergraduate Fees**	
From working-class homes:	22.8%	Fees for UK/EU students:	£3,290
		International Student fees:	£10,100-£12,765

Cass Business School (City University London)
Tel. +442070405060; www.city.ac.uk

Student Name:
Yousif Al Murbat

IB World School:
Naseem International School

Nationality:
Bahraini

What course do you currently study?
Investment and Financial Risk Management, Third Year

University offer:
35

How does your workload at university compare to the IB Diploma?

The workload during the first year of university was much less compared to the final year of IB. What I found was that most students who had studied A-levels had struggled with several core modules in comparison to the ones who had completed the IB. For instance, I ended up devoting less study time for modules such as Introduction to Economics and Quantitative Methods than several students. In terms of the second year, the workload was on the same level as the IB while the third year was definitely harder and more time consuming. The majority of my time was devoted towards writing a 10,000 word dissertation. I found that the IB's EE does prepare students for both their final year project as well as the courseworks which were completed throughout the three years at university.

Would you say you have an advantage over A-Level students in your studies? How?

I definitely would agree that A-level students are at a disadvantage when starting university. The IB allows students to have an overall better level of understanding in terms of how to write structured essays, construct projects and deliver presentations. What was immediately apparent was that A-level students all found it difficult to go about writing long essays (2000-2500 words), which for an IB student was typical of an internal assessment. Moreover, the ability to use several Microsoft Office tools - mainly Word, Excel and PowerPoint - was quite low for A-level students. As my course involves a large chunk of Excel and Word usage, I found myself at a larger advantage and still do even after three years.

Is there any element of the IB that you have found particularly useful in your university studies?

In my opinion the Extended Essay was the most beneficial assignment of the IB as it provides an introduction to how university work is actually carried out. The EE allows for students to gain the skills of conducting their individual long term research projects and teaches them how to structure long essays with minimal assistance. I also think that CAS is very important when applying to jobs and enables university students to stand out as more successful and well-rounded candidates. I personally found it very useful to use examples from my CAS experiences during interviews.

Did you find your personal requirements fair? Do you feel the offer under/overrated the IB system?

I felt that for Cass a 35 was appropriate for the course I am doing. But generally I do feel that universities ask for higher IB requirements than necessary especially in terms of A-level points. I think in general the IB is underrated in the UK and several universities admissions do not understand the large difference between the IB diploma and A-levels.

How does the social life compare to the one you had at school?
Both my social life at university and at school have been very enjoyable. Nevertheless, I do still keep in contact with several students form my old school and I find that the friendships I made at school will be more long term than the ones at university.

Are there special efforts made to accommodate international students?
I am not aware of any special efforts made at my university to accommodate any international students. There are international societies but I have never taken great interest in them.

Are there many former IB students? Do you socialize with them?
There are several former IB students at my university - mostly from Europe. I do socialize with a lot of them as they generally are more international and I find that their background and lifestyle is more similar to mine than A-level students.

Would you recommend your university to prospective IB students?
I would definitely recommend Cass Business School to prospective IB students. Although the organization of the university has not been as how I'd expect, the people you meet at Cass are very similar to the people you would meet at your typical IB school. The overall experience has been great and I've found that the IB has helped in both academic as well as social aspects of my university career so far.

Further Statistics and Information

Students		Accommodation	
Undergraduates:	**8,050**	University-provided places:	1,360
Postgraduates:	**4,265**	Percentage catered:	0%
Overseas students:	**15.6%**	Self-catered costs (per week):	£106-£195
Applications per place:	**7.9**		
From state-sector schools:	**92.5%**	**Undergraduate Fees**	
From working-class homes:	**39.6%**	Fees for UK/EU students:	£3,290
		International Student fees:	£8,900-£11,500

University of Central Lancashire

Tel. +441772892400; enquiries@uclan.ac.uk; www.uclan.ac.uk

Student Name:
Fredrik Karlsson

IB World School:
IT-Gymnasiet, Skövde

Nationality:
Swedish

What course do you currently study?
First year, Law

University offer:
28 points

How does your workload at university compare to the IB Diploma?

So far, the Law coursework has not been as much work as the IB was. However, I am still in my first semester at university and I'm sure the workload will increase over the coming months. Still, I feel that the IB prepares you well for the coursework as you are used to a heavy workload.

Would you say you have an advantage over A-Level students in your studies? How?

In my opinion, I do believe that IB students have an advantage over A-level students as we are both used to the heavy workload of the IB, as well as writing essays and dissertations. I think IB students here find the coursework less stressful as they are used to the pressure, and we are more familiar with the types of tasks we are set as part of the coursework.

Is there any element of the IB that you have found particularly useful in your university studies?

Personally, I feel that IB History has helped me a great deal, especially when it comes to coursework and source analysis in essays. A large part of the Law course is reading and analysing case law, and the approach is very similar to what you are taught in IB History. Extended Essay also prepares you well for writing university dissertations and longer essays in the course, which I feel that some A-level students don't have a lot of experience in.

Did you find your personal requirements fair? Do you feel the offer under/overrated the IB system?

At first I thought the offer I received underrated the IB programme, but after discussing offers with A-level students on my course, I also realized that it's difficult to compare offers between the IB and A-levels. After the first semester of the course, I think my personal requirements were fair, and suitable for the course.

How does the social life compare to the one you had at school?

The social life at UCLan is incredible, it's so easy to meet new people, and since the university is such a big part of Preston, there are always student nights out. Staying in university halls also makes it easier to meet people when you first arrive.

Are there special efforts made to accommodate international students?

Moving to Preston as an international student was easier than I had imagined. There is always help available, and the Student Union and Student Liaison Officers are there to help the students settle in.

Are there many former IB students? Do you socialize with them?

Most of the students I meet are former A-level students, but I have met a few IB students over the past few months. The ones I have met agree that the IB prepares you well for university, and that the IB was more difficult and much more work than the university coursework.

Would you recommend your university to prospective IB students?

Definitely, it's a great university and a great town to live in for students. It's very international, so you will meet people from all over the world, and you are more than likely to meet someone from your own country too. The social life is amazing, it's easy to meet people and make new friends. The Law course is better than I expected, and personally, I really enjoy it and feel it was the right move for me.

Further Statistics and Information

Students		Accommodation	
Undergraduates:	**16,265**	University-provided places:	2,000
Postgraduates:	**1,235**	Percentage catered:	0%
Overseas students:	**10.2%**	Self-catered costs (per week):	£75-£90
Applications per place:	**3.7**		
From state-sector schools:	**97.9%**	**Undergraduate Fees**	
From working-class homes:	**43.7%**	Fees for UK/EU students:	£3,290
		International Student fees:	£8,900 - £9,500

Central Saint Martins (University of the Arts)
Tel. +4420 7514 6130; www.arts.ac.uk

Student Name:
Dimitri Hadjichristou

IB World School:
International School of Luxembourg

Nationality:
Greek

What course do you currently study?
Foundation Year

University offer:
UC

How does your workload at university compare to the IB Diploma?

Personally I felt the workload I had in my foundation made I.B.'s workload seem like a piece of cake.

Would you say you have an advantage over A-Level students in your studies? How?

No, not necessarily, art schools prefer A-level students because they take fewer subjects and have far more time to focus on their artwork than I.B. students.

Is there any element of the IB that you have found particularly useful in your university studies?

Not particularly, no.

Did you find your personal requirements fair? Do you feel the offer under/overrated the IB system?

I was a little disappointed, I felt like the university didn't really care about all the hard work I was putting into my I.B. as Central Saint Martins only really care about artistic talent, nothing else.

How does the social life compare to the one you had at school?

I didn't particularly have a great time socially in my school as I didn't get along with my fellow seniors. However I played basketball and my teammates were my best friends, we would always hang out together. At university I didn't enjoy the social life for several reasons, there's no campus, most of the students have lived in London all their life so they hang out with their high school/childhood friends outside of university hours, and also Saint Martins itself was very cliquey so I didn't enjoy it too much. However, my friend played on the girl's hockey team and loved Saint Martins socially.

Are there special efforts made to accommodate international students?

Yes there are societies, for example I joined the basketball society but I quit shortly after because since it was an arts university, we didn't have a gym so we had to train at Southbank and various other facilities and commuting and training times became a pain. It seems there are lots of societies but the students have to make a lot more effort to become a part of them. There were lots of student events and organisations running them. There was also a lot of student support offered through the University and a large student union. All of the student halls for the University of the Arts were full of students from all over the world.

Are there many former IB students? Do you socialize with them?

Yeah there were a few. I socialised with a few of them but not all the time. Because it was so international there were students from all kinds of academic backgrounds. Although most had completed A-levels, I did tend to socialise with some IB students however most of them were at different campuses/colleges within the University of the Arts London, most of which I met living in Halls. At CSM I would say the majority were A-level students with a few exceptions.

Would you recommend your university to prospective IB students?

Yes, I would recommend my university to I.B. students because educationally it's an incredible place to study and it's an epicentre of the creative arts where extraordinary things take place. Although at the same time I would warn them that they have to make the effort themselves to enjoy it socially.

Further Statistics and Information [University of the Arts, London]

Students		Accommodation	
Undergraduates:	16,265	University-provided places:	2,000
Postgraduates:	1,270	Percentage catered:	0%
Overseas students:	10.2%	Self-catered costs:	£75-£90 a week
Applications per place:	3.7		
From state-sector schools:	97.9%	**Undergraduate Fees**	
From working-class homes:	43.7%	Fees for UK/EU students:	£3,290
		International Student fees:	£9,000-£9,500

Durham University
Tel. +441913346123; www.dur.ac.uk

Student Name:
Sofia Carlsson

IB World School:
United World College (Singapore)

Nationality:
Swedish

What course do you currently study?
Molecular Biology

University offer:
37

How does your workload at university compare to the IB Diploma?
As Durham is a pretty traditional university, the classes are always in small groups and assessment is usually by written examinations. Personally, I found IB to be more difficult because you had to juggle six subjects – some of which you had no real interest in. At university, you are studying something you wanted to do for 3 years, so in that sense the workload feels lighter and more enjoyable

Would you say you have an advantage over A-Level students in your studies? How?
To a certain extent, yes. I often find that I am much more flexible at following instructions and carrying out procedures in comparison to my A-level peers. Also, coping with stress and late nights is not as much of a problem to me as it is for some of my friends.

Is there any element of the IB that you have found particularly useful in your university studies?
Certainly for those studying sciences, the lab reports and procedures carried out during IB are very useful. Also, I am better able to handle bibliographies and citations in comparison to the other peers – and for this I largely have the Extended Essay to thank. The IB also taught me to fear examinations less – and the exam coping techniques I learned in highschool are all still very important to me at university level.

Did you find your personal requirements fair? Do you feel the offer under/overrated the IB system?

If I were to make a direct comparison to the A-level requirements, then yes, I do feel that the university was asking more from me then from other students.

However, that being said, I think top universities asking for 3 A's at A-level will struggle to differentiate between candidates because so many of them are capable of achieving that. In this sense, the IB crowd may be at an advantage.

How does the social life compare to the one you had at school?

Durham town can be pretty lively, and the university integrates perfectly with local surroundings. For those looking for a bit more adventure or a change of scene, Newcastle is a very short train journey away.

Are there special efforts made to accommodate international students?

Given that nearly one out of 10 students is from abroad, the university does have overseas representatives to help out with any issues. Also, there are societies that students can join. Your best bet for meeting students from abroad if you don't have any on your course would be to join a sports team. Durham has very strong rowing, rugby and hockey teams.

Are there many former IB students? Do you socialize with them?

Not too many, but I have bumped into a few. I find that integrating with the local culture and living the typical 'British' university life is more appealing than sticking with the ex-IB crowd.

Would you recommend your university to prospective IB students?

Certainly. Durham constantly ranks among the top universities for student satisfaction and for academic achievement. It is a collegiate system, meaning that you should probably research your prospective college before applying anywhere to see what it is really like. The university boasts impressive alumni, including Andrew Strauss and Will Greenwood. Any IB student applying to Durham would not regret their decision.

Further Statistics and Information

Students		Accommodation	
Undergraduates:	11,145	University-provided places:	5,758
Postgraduates:	3,800	Percentage catered:	67%
Overseas students:	8.6%	Self-catered costs (per week):	£80-£100
Applications per place:	6.5		
From state-sector schools:	59.2%	**Undergraduate Fees**	
From working-class homes:	16.8%	Fees for UK/EU students:	£3,290
		International Student fees:	£12,400-£14,865

University of Edinburgh
Tel. +441316511905; www.ed.ac.uk

Student Name:
Eivand Omli

IB World School:
International School of The Hague

Nationality:
Norwegian

What course do you currently study?
4th year, B.Sc. (Hons) Biomedical Sciences (Pharmacology)

University offer:
32

How does your workload at university compare to the IB Diploma?

My workload at university is smaller to that of the IB Diploma. The workload of the IB Diploma was greater in the sense that we needed to take 6 subjects which all had weekly deadlines. At university the deadlines are longer and the lectures much shorter, however there is a greater deal of self-study involved.

Would you say you have an advantage over A-Level students in your studies? How?

I believe the IB Diploma gives you a great advantage over students with A-levels. The need to take 6 subjects, three of them at higher level, which must include a math, a science and a foreign language. This gives a much broader academic background compared to the A levels, thus your options are much broader when applying for universities.

Is there any element of the IB that you have found particularly useful in your university studies?
The Extended Essay was a good preparation essay writing at university. Many other students who have not taken the IB had difficulties writing longer essays, thus the Extended Essay gave me a good advantage over others. The higher level science subjects (Physics and Chemistry) prepared me well for a science degree at university. Much of what was taught in the first year we had already covered in depth in the IB.

Did you find your personal requirements fair? Do you feel the offer under/overrated the IB system?

I found that the personal requirements fair and that the offer valued the requirements of the IB system.

How does the social life compare to the one you had at school?

The social life at university is very different from the one I had at school. There is much more free time at university especially during the week and thus you end up going out much more during the week rather than the weekend which was common at school. As you live with and meet so many different people there is always something going on and always a place to go out.

Are there special efforts made to accommodate international students?

There are an endless amount of societies representing almost every country across the globe, which have weekly social events where you can meet students from your own country or countries you have lived in, finding many students with a similar background to yours. There are overseas representatives and an international student office which can help you with any concerns. Thus, the university accommodates international students very well.

Are there many former IB students? Do you socialize with them?

There are many former IB students at the university. It is easy to engage and socialise with them as they have the similar international background and experiences as I have.

Would you recommend your university to prospective IB students?

I would definitely recommend University of Edinburgh to prospective IB students. There is a large international student body and the city is also very international. The university is highly regarded worldwide and leaves you with a great degree and future opportunities. The rigour of the IB program also prepares you to do well here.

Further Statistics and Information

Students		Accommodation	
Undergraduates:	16,590	University-provided places:	6,300
Postgraduates:	5,200	Percentage catered:	30%
Overseas students:	15.0%	Self-catered costs (per week):	£150-£190
Applications per place:	8.6		
From state-sector schools:	70.8%	**Undergraduate Fees**	
From working-class homes:	18.6%	Fees for UK/EU students:	£3,290
		International Student fees:	£11,600-£15,200

University of Essex

Tel. +44 1206 873778; www.essex.ac.uk

Student Name:
Floris Schatz

IB World School:
Ecole Internationale de Geneve

Nationality:
Dutch

What course do you currently study?
Economics, Finalist

University offer:
31

How does your workload at university compare to the IB Diploma?

On average the compulsory workload is far less. However, every few weeks come the essay/project periods. All your work is well organized to be due in the same week or two so that every now and then you're locked in the library for hours on end.

Would you say you have an advantage over A-Level students in your studies? How?

Having taken Maths Higher, the first year of University was a piece of cake. Two points off a first (made a stupid mistake in one important exam) with next to no studying. However, this mind-set carried over to second year where the work was not so easy, causing my grades to drop. Still, IB is advantageous if you're not lazy like me.

Is there any element of the IB that you have found particularly useful in your university studies?

Maths Higher, but that may be due to that one particular teacher.

Did you find your personal requirements fair? Do you feel the offer under/overrated the IB system?

Under-rated. IB requires six subjects, where A-level students can get by with just three. IB is known to be more difficult, but even a 1 in 100, 000 perfect score of 45 equalled something like 6 A's. But, I heard this was changing lately – my experience may be outdated.

How does the social life compare to the one you had at school?

Every IB student was accused at some point in their early University life of being prejudiced. This stems from an international school where nobody really cares what colour your skin is and everyone feels comfortable making jokes about it. Also, there's a lot more going out. Social and sporting facilities are all adequate, with the sports centre and the students' union bar both undergoing refurbishment recently. There are now four bars, an enlarged and refurbished nightclub and numerous cafes on campus.

Are there special efforts made to accommodate international students?

Yes, but I never bothered as they only served to alienate people from the majority of other students. Most of the cliques at University were race/ethnicity based. With regards to assistance to overseas students, the university does guarantee accommodation to anyone from abroad – which is rather nice if you are from the other side of the world.

Are there many former IB students? Do you socialize with them?

Statistics said there were, but I never met any. I socialized with whoever seemed friendly and shared interests with me.

Would you recommend your university to prospective IB students?

The University is rated well for certain subjects, with requirements that aren't too high. I found that most of the teachers leave much to be desired. You are usually better off studying on your own and skipping the lectures – which may suit some a lot more than others. Certain degrees rank a lot higher for Essex than others, and you should make sure to check out how well-taught your specific interest area is before making any final decisions.

Further Statistics and Information

Students		Accommodation	
Undergraduates:	7,945	University-provided places:	4,166
Postgraduates:	1,805	Percentage catered:	0%
Overseas students:	20.1%	Self-catered costs (per week):	£65-£125
Applications per place:	4.3		
From state-sector schools:	96.1%	**Undergraduate Fees**	
From working-class homes:	38.9%	Fees for UK/EU students:	£3,290
		International Student fees:	£9,250-£11,990

University of Exeter

Tel. +441392 263855; www.exeter.ac.uk

Student Name:
Tina Rosso

IB World School:
International School of Turin

Nationality:
Italian

What course do you currently study?
Accounting and Finance

University offer:
36, 5 in Math SL

How does your workload at university compare to the IB Diploma?

Exeter is a pretty tough university, so the amount of work every week is rather overwhelming. That being said, nothing quite compares to the pain and suffering of the two year IB program.

Would you say you have an advantage over A-Level students in your studies? How?

This is not something I noticed in the first few weeks but depending on which course you study there will come times when you have covered some things in more depth than your peers. This is especially true for math-based courses because math is not compulsory for A-level students.

Is there any element of the IB that you have found particularly useful in your university studies?

Certainly the IB experience as a whole has helped me greatly in coping with deadlines and juggling several assignments at a time. Business and Management were very helpful for my degree, as well as the experience of already having written a mini-thesis in the form of the Extended Essay.

Did you find your personal requirements fair? Do you feel the offer under/overrated the IB system?

It seemed a bit too much if I'm being honest. Also, the Exeter prospectus suggested that most IB offers were between 33-35 when in reality most of my friends got offers of 36+ which was a bit surprising. Compared to the A-levels, I certainly feel the offer underrated the IB system.

How does the social life compare to the one you had at school?

Exeter is great with regards to nightlife and clubs/societies. Of course, the typical university experience in the UK will be very different from that of what most IB students enjoyed in their highschool (mostly because you are in a sort of IB 'bubble' and you spend your weekend with your classmates only). At university there are far more opportunities to have a wide range of friends, and it is certainly less cliquey than school. Exeter has a great Student Union, and Fresher's week will be one of your favourite times ever.

Are there special efforts made to accommodate international students?

There are several thousand students from abroad and it is very welcoming to see them spread across campus. Exeter in itself is not a very international city, but things such as the International Society and the Erasmus Society have made the experience much more pleasant. Students seem to be happy, although some do wish for even more multiculturalism.

Are there many former IB students? Do you socialize with them?

There are a few on my course who happen to be in my close circle of friends but I would not say that Exeter is among the most popular choices for IB students

Would you recommend your university to prospective IB students?

The Exeter experience is what the university really leverages on. There are beautiful surroundings and a great mixture of city and countryside life. Also there is good weather (for the UK anyhow) coupled with great teaching and sporting facilities in an American-like campus. It is one of the most vibrant student experiences and I highly recommend it.

Further Statistics and Information

Students		Accommodation	
Undergraduates:	**11,065**	University-provided places:	4,309
Postgraduates:	**3,276**	Percentage catered:	37%
Overseas students:	**7.8%**	Self-catered costs (per week):	£73-£124
Applications per place:	**6.8**		
From state-sector schools:	**71.0%**	**Undergraduate Fees**	
From working-class homes:	**20.8%**	Fees for UK/EU students:	£3,290
		International Student fees:	£11,000-£13,200

European Business School (Regents College)

Tel. +44 207 487 7700+44; www.regents.ac.uk

Student Name:
Constantijn Huynen

IB World School:
International School of Amsterdam

Nationality:
Dutch

What course do you currently study?
International Business Management

University offer:
30

How does your workload at university compare to the IB Diploma?

The total work at university was more however, due to less class time I spent more hours on IB work. My university was more project-based, with periods of being very busy, and other periods having nothing to do. During the IB I felt more pressure due to a consistently large workload.

Would you say you have an advantage over A-Level students in your studies? How?

Yes. When comparing my results at university to those students who did A levels, I got higher grades, as did the other IB students. Also the critical thinking promoted by the IB gave an advantage as this is more comparable to what the university expects.

Is there any element of the IB that you have found particularly useful in your university studies?

The Extended Essay and Business Management course were very helpful for me.

Did you find your personal requirements fair? Do you feel the offer under/overrated the IB system?

I believe my offer was far from fair. Considering that all IB students systematically achieved higher marks, I truly believe the A levels were over rated.

How does the social life compare to the one you had at school?

There are two big differences in the social lives. First, at university you choose the friends you hang out with, while at school of course you have your good friends but because of the large contact time you have at school with everyone you tend to socialise with whoever is in your class. Second, at university you aren't bound by parents, class time or anything. It is absolutely your life to do and choose what you like. This changes your perception.

Are there special efforts made to accommodate international students?

Because I went to Regents, there are nearly only international students, so everything is done to accommodate us. It's very important to the university, but few students actually make use of this and prefer to do their own thing in London.

Are there many former IB students? Do you socialize with them?

I think there were about 15% of the students that did IB. It's not because they did IB you socialise with them but somehow through natural selection you do tend to meet the IB students, become friends and then realise you both did IB.

Would you recommend your university to prospective IB students?

I would, if they are prepared to make the effort because they want to succeed. Regents is great for teaching practical skills which you need in day to day business, but is easy to pass. Therefore the aim must be to be the best of the year, then it will teach you valuable skills. It also gives you an easier start in the job market, as well as being a great place for contacts.

Further Statistics and Information

Students		Accommodation	
Undergraduates:	**N/A**	University-provided places:	N/A
Postgraduates:	**N/A**	Percentage catered:	N/A
Overseas students:	**N/A**	Self-catered costs (per week):	N/A
Applications per place:	**N/A**		
From state-sector schools:	**N/A**	**Undergraduate Fees**	
From working-class homes:	**N/A**	Fees for UK/EU students:	N/A
		International Student fees:	N/A

Imperial College of Science, Technology and Medicine
Tel. +442075948014; www.imperial.ac.uk

Student Name:
Gonzalo de Gisbert

IB World School
American International School of Johannesburg

What course do you currently study?
4th Year, Electrical Engineering with Management

University offer
38 Points with 6 Maths HL, 6 Physics HL, 5 English HL/SL

How does your workload at university compare to the IB Diploma?
During the first year it compared quite closely in terms of the amount of work which I had each week for modules. However, I also had electrical labs and computing labs which added a bit more to the work load. Overall it was manageable without too much of an adjustment. I had 9 modules/subjects for EEE first year. Second year however, the workload increased significantly compared to what I had ever had to do for IB. Having undergone the IB, I suppose I was somewhat prepared to adjust/accommodate for sudden increases in work load from what I was used to, but it definitely was a lot more than IB. This is also taking into account second year I had 13 different modules I took, each of which had either a 2 or 3 hour exam in the Summer Term. IB I had multiple papers per subject but I only had 6 subjects. Third and Fourth year the work load has increased furthermore so there isn't much point comparing to IB anymore because I am fairly certain I didn't spend about 12-15 hours on 4-5 days a week.

Would you say you have an advantage over A-Level students in your studies? How?
I think the advantage I have was the fact that I had to take as a pre-requisite HL Maths for Engineering whereas for A Level, Imperial did not require Further Maths which was comparable to the Options for Math HL. For this I suppose I had an advantage over the people that had only undertaken simple A Level Maths. In terms of the workload, A level students typically only take 3-4 A level subjects while IB students had to take 6 subjects, which were not all necessarily related to our degree (Language A, B + social studies in my case). In A level, an advantage I suppose they had was that they could specialize to what they were going to study.

Is there any element of the IB that you have found particularly useful in your university studies?
I think that the Extended Essay did well in teaching one how to write a concise report on a particular topic. In school, writing a 4000 word report seemed daunting but after overcoming the Extended Essay, writing reports between 3000-5000 words (which is quite common) does not seem that daunting anymore. ToK was not of particular use to my degree, I suppose only in the way in made you think of things "outside the box" which could always be considered useful for an engineer. Subject wise I was at quite a disadvantage because the Electrical/Electronics section in IB Physics was extremely poor in regards to what many A Level Physics students had learnt.

Did you find your personal requirements fair? Do you feel the offer under/overrated the IB system?
I found my personal requirements fair overall. A 6 in Maths HL and Physics HL was realistic because had one received anything lower, I think they would have had significant trouble in the first two years of EEE since the increase in difficulty, in particular for the Maths, was even very challenging for me and I missed a 7 by 5 points. In terms of Physics, if I am honest it was quite irrelevant for the topics studied in HL Physics related to my degree.

How does the social life compare to the one you had at school?

It is quite different in that you obviously have the whole living "alone" thing in uni while in school I did not. With IB, once I had finished school for the day I would do sports in the afternoon and then just come home. Do work, eat dinner, and then more work. Weekends I would see my friends, but I suppose I had the whole parental guidance/consciousness as well. In addition, with the IB, going to an American School I had quizzes and tests every week which kept me a lot more on top of my work. In university I have a lot of course works to do, but most of my problem sheets are optional and thus I tend to not do them until exam revision. This yields more free time due to the fact that I do not HAVE to work, hence I would rather go to the pub. In uni, I also have a lot less classes then at school where it was 7-15h everyday so I always fit seeing friends in between.

Are there special efforts made to accommodate international students?

Although I am considered an International Student simply because I grew up in South Africa/Applied from a South African school I hold a Spanish Passport and thus tend to ignore all international students welfare help, e-mails, etc. In terms of societies and social events, seeing as there is a large Asian population at Imperial, I would say there is a very high activity by overseas students and lots of societies for them.

Are there many former IB students? Do you socialize with them?

I have met a few IB students at my university, but our conversations have typically just involved the shock of "Oh you did IB too?!?!? What did you get???". But other than this, I would not say I interact or socialise with them any differently. I have noticed though there are very few people who do the IB in comparison to people who have done A Levels. This is also including Asian students from Singapore, Malaysia, and China etc. who regardless of being international, have done the A Level System.

Would you recommend your university to prospective IB students?

Of course! I think Imperial is a great school to come and study. I have only studied one of several degrees they have in engineering/science but I still find it to be a school with very high quality of teaching and research. It is also well known in the UK which is always useful for job applications. Being one of the top engineering schools in the UK/Europe I personally prefer the degree system for engineering to those of Oxbridge (other two leading institutions) where you have to do general engineering and only really specialize in your last two years. For Imperial, you specialize and go into much more detail from the start. I base this evidence on speaking with friends from Cambridge who in the second year did many similar modules of Electronics as we did, however ours covered many more sections/topics than theirs since their Electronics Module was one of various topics, with others being Mechanical, Chemical, Aeronautical Etc.

Further Statistics and Information

Students		Accommodation	
Undergraduates:	8,580	University-provided places:	2,497
Postgraduates:	4,345	Percentage catered:	0%
Overseas students:	34.7%	Self-catered costs:	£55-£220 a week
Applications per place:	5.9		
From state-sector schools:	62.1%	**Undergraduate Fees**	
From working-class homes:	18.7%	Fees for UK/EU students:	£3,290
		International Student fees:	£19,800–£21,850

University of Kent
Tel. +441227827272; www.kent.ac.uk

Student Name:
George Jurgens

IB World School:
International School of Luxembourg

Nationality:
Dutch

What course do you currently study?
Final year (Year 4) of Business Administration with Studies in Asia

University offer:
33 points total

How does your workload at university compare to the IB Diploma?

1st year was especially easy, and made me lazy as workload was minimal compared to IB program. I felt I was one step ahead of most students. Following into 2nd and 3rd (officially my 4th year after a year abroad) you can tell a difference between International Students (mostly IB) and A-level students, especially when it comes down to independent thinking and group work - IB students being more serious and harder workers, able to delegate work, and work more effectively. A-level students, or generally UK students tend to hinder group work, and bring group marks down due to lack of presentation skills, and poor participation in class/group discussions (despite it being in their native language)

Would you say you have an advantage over A-Level students in your studies? How?

Yes. I feel I'm more competent at in-class presentations and discussions. I tend to notice mostly international students (of which I assume most are IB students) are more likely to engage in class discussions with seminar leaders.

Is there any element of the IB that you have found particularly useful in your university studies?
The extended essay and internal assessments of the IB reflect the quantity and quality of reports/essays demanded by universities, where we may have a greater development in independent thinking and ability to research information better than A-level students. Presentation's (although not strictly a part of the IB) at International School's have been beneficial to my university studies. Instilled better confidence and greater abilities in presenting to other pupils

Did you find your personal requirements fair? Do you feel the offer under/overrated the IB system?
I don't know the A-level system too well and am not sure how they quantify the differences in scores as a means of benchmarking entry requirements for universities. But generally I feel the IB is still lacking acceptance by universities, underestimating IB scoring system.

How does the social life compare to the one you had at school?

1st year on Campus is great – there are many bars and restaurants on campus. Going into your second year, you may feel you are repeating a lot of the same nights, with only a few clubs around Canterbury, as it's mostly a 'pub city'. There are very many societies, and these will make your social life much more interesting - to my regret I did not get involved in these until my final year.

Are there special efforts made to accommodate international students?

The University of Kent classifies themselves as the European University of England - mostly due to its favourable location to Dover/Folkston ferry/Eurotunnel crossing into France, and its satellite campuses in Brussels and I think Paris. As I'm classified as an EU student, I don't fall under the International student's category. However to my knowledge there is an International Students 'organization' aimed at aiding international students in the first year of arrival to integrate, socialize etc.

Are there many former IB students? Do you socialize with them?

I've come across a few, from school's I've been a part of in the past. It appears most are doing International Business rather than Business Administration. I socialize with the ones I knew from before university, but there doesn't seem to be a society or social-sphere for IB students.

Would you recommend your university to prospective IB students?

There are great opportunities for exchange programs with my university (although not very well publicized to current students) It's a great campus university, but if you are used to a fast-passed city lifestyle then Canterbury may not be your best choice. It's a pub city, with only a few clubs. But its proximity to London (High-speed train from Canterbury to London in 56mins) makes it easy to get away when you want to. It's a great midway location between London and the rest of Europe. You will find many EU students at the university, creating a great diversity of students.

Further Statistics and Information

Students		Accommodation	
Undergraduates:	11,920	University-provided places:	4,300
Postgraduates:	1,395	Percentage catered:	18%
Overseas students:	13.5%	Self-catered costs (per week):	£90-£128
Applications per place:	4.8		
From state-sector schools:	93.2%	**Undergraduate Fees**	
From working-class homes:	28.3%	Fees for UK/EU students:	£3,290
		International Student fees:	£10,350-£12,590

King's College London
Tel. +442078487070; www.kcl.ac.uk

Student Name:
Giulia Rinaldi

IB World School:
United World College of South East Asia

Nationality:
Italian

What course do you currently study?
Second year, Nursing

University offer:
Unconditional

How does your workload at university compare to the IB Diploma?

The workload is much less than the IB was. It is probably about half of the IB at least compared to the grade 12 workload. The answer to this question will vary depending on which course you study at Kings – some of my medic friends rarely see the light of day. It would be wise to do some research into specific courses before deciding what you want to study.

Would you say you have an advantage over A-Level students in your studies? How?

Yes, because I had to take 6 subjects and I have a much wider range of knowledge. Especially when it comes to math subjects I find a lot of my class mates dropped math and are now having to catch up in much less time. Moreover, TOK helped with many of university essays which include "discussions" of topics in my modules.

Is there any element of the IB that you have found particularly useful in your university studies?

Yes, as aforementioned TOK was particularly helpful, as well as the experience of writing a lengthy essay.

Did you find your personal requirements fair? Do you feel the offer under/overrated the IB system?

I felt that the University under rated the IB system. I believe that A-levels are still regarded at higher or as equal as the IB, whilst, in my opinion the IB should be rated higher.

How does the social life compare to the one you had at school?

The social life is more or less the same as the one I had at school. For me social life is a personal choice and you can choose to have as much as you want of it in your life.

Living in London, you really are spoilt for choice with regards to clubs, societies and culture. It has everything and anything that you like

Are there special efforts made to accommodate international students?

Yes, there are societies of many nationalities. It really is up to you with regards to how involved you wish to get in the various societies and clubs that Kings has to offer.

Are there many former IB students? Do you socialize with them?

In my course there are not so I do not socialize with them. I am doing Nursing and it is a very local subject. That being said, my first year accommodation was in the Nido building in Kings Cross and there seemed to be a large number of former IB kids residing there.

Would you recommend your university to prospective IB students?

Yes I love King's college. It is in London and it is in a great location and there is something going on every night and most people are very international and open minded. Kings is one of the oldest and largest of the London universities and continuously ranks very highly amongst university rankings. An amazing place to live your last teenage years and early twenties!

Further Statistics and Information

Students		Accommodation	
Undergraduates:	**12,085**	University-provided places:	2,654
Postgraduates:	**4,690**	Percentage catered:	18%
Overseas students:	**15.2%**	Self-catered costs (per week):	£115
Applications per place:	**8.4**		
From state-sector schools:	**72.6%**	**Undergraduate Fees**	
From working-class homes:	**24.2%**	Fees for UK/EU students:	£3,290
		International Student fees:	£12,500 - £15,800

London College of Fashion (University of the Arts)

Tel. +4420 7514 6130; info@arts.ac.uk; www.arts.ac.uk

Student Name:
Asia Dwyer

IB World School
International School of Rotterdam

Nationality:
Canadian/Philippines

What course do you currently study?
First year. Access to Higher Education [Fashion]

University offer
Unconditional

How does your workload at university compare to the IB Diploma?

After completing the IB Diploma, I have found the workload at university a lot easier to handle. Although it is slightly heavier, I have found that through the IB I have learnt the importance of time management which has made my first year much easier. Also, the workload feels much lighter as I am studying a course which I enjoy 100%, with all subjects relevant to my future, whereas in the IB, there were many subjects which I struggled with.

Would you say you have an advantage over A-Level students in your studies? How?

The most important class within my course is called Fashion Portfolio, in which we solely work on our art notebook. This notebook consists of all our research, experiments, and ideas we have relevant to the assignment given at the beginning of the year. This shows our thought process, how we are able to connect different ideas together and eventually create a final collection. It is crucial that we do extremely well in this notebook as it makes up the majority of our portfolios which we will use to apply for our BA next year. It is in this class particularly where I have realized the advantages which I have over A-level students. As throughout the two years of the IB, I had to prepare the same type of notebook, I have found myself ahead of the class. I was able to begin my art book immediately and correctly, versus other students who struggled to understand what exactly was meant to be done. Because I was able to understand the concept of the art book from the beginning, it has been a very enjoyable experience and I found myself achieving double the amount of work than the other students.

Is there any element of the IB that you have found particularly useful in your university studies?

Studying at the University of the Arts, I have found that taking Art at a higher level as well as writing my extended essay about art and fashion, I have had an advantage over the students who did not complete the IB diploma. Taking art at a higher level made me more aware of both art history as well as art today. Mandatory visits to exhibitions and galleries, travelling to other countries with my art class, and recording every step of the way has made me a stronger art student. I have found that the majority of the students I am currently studying are not yet as open minded as I have become due to the IB. The extended essay was also useful, not only because of all I had learnt through the research, but getting used to writing essays of a large word count.

Did you find your personal requirements fair? Do you feel the offer under/overrated the IB system?

I was very pleased with fairness of the requirements for this course. IB was a very tough experience for me, but as the conditions were to perform well at the interview and pass the IB, I was felt confident when applying.

How does the social life compare to the one you had at school?

Coming from international schools throughout middle and high school, consisting of maximum 500 students, I have found that it has been easier socially. There is roughly double the amount of people to socialize with, all sharing the same interests, therefor, spending time with friends is something I look forward to rather than having to make an effort as I did in high school. It has also been refreshing to be in such a competitive environment and learning and sharing ideas with fellow students. This was something I rarely came across in high school.

Are there special efforts made to accommodate international students?

No, I am not aware of any extra efforts made in my university. This is something the school should improve on as I have noticed many of the international students struggling. I, however, have enjoyed making at effort to meet people international or not, and have met a wide range of people and learned much from them.

Are there many former IB students? Do you socialize with them?

So far in my university experience, I have only met a few IB students. I have socialized with them, and all of them have been overconfident and obviously aware of the advantages which they have over the other students. The former IB students I have met have not been pleasant.

Would you recommend your university to prospective IB students?

I would recommend my foundation course for students who are interested in studying fashion in the future, but hesitant of which part of the industry to pursue. The course is intense, however, it has been helpful to lead me in the right direction of what specific course to study for my BA next year. The university has also helped me explore new aspects of the industry which I was unaware of before and have made me feel that my possibilities are endless.

Further Statistics and Information [University of the Arts, London]

Students		Accommodation	
Undergraduates:	16,265	University-provided places:	2,000
Postgraduates:	1,270	Percentage catered:	0%
Overseas students:	10.2%	Self-catered costs:	£75-£90 a week
Applications per place:	3.7		
From state-sector schools:	97.9%	**Undergraduate Fees**	
From working-class homes:	43.7%	Fees for UK/EU students:	£3,290
		International Student fees:	£9,000-£9,500

London College of Communications (Uni of the Arts)
Tel. +44207514 6130; www.arts.ac.uk

Student Name:
Athena De Belder

IB World School:
Antwerp International School

Nationality:
Belgian

What course do you currently study?
Journalism

University offer:
28, 6 in English

How does your workload at university compare to the IB Diploma?

There is a similar workload but different way of approaching work and assignments – more creative freedom and personal touch.

Would you say you have an advantage over A-Level students in your studies? How?

Yes, in terms of essay writing and general knowledge of various subjects. I feel that I am better at structuring my arguments and having a more coherent thought process than some of my peers.

Is there any element of the IB that you have found particularly useful in your university studies?

Not particularly, no.

Did you find your personal requirements fair? Do you feel the offer under/overrated the IB system?

For me the requirements were easy to fulfil. I am not too sure what the A-level requirements are, or any other qualifications.

How does the social life compare to the one you had at school?

There is a greater variety of people and social activities. University life in London is incomparable to the life you have at school. Life in London is much more independent and very busy but fun. The great thing is that you don't necessarily have to constantly hang out with university friends. I still see school friends on a weekly basis, especially the ones that continued their studies in London.

Are there special efforts made to accommodate international students?

Not in particular. I am not too involved with the university societies. This seems like something that you need to seek out if you want to get involved – there will be no student reps knocking on your door encouraging you to join any society.

Are there many former IB students? Do you socialize with them?

Not many IB students. I don't necessarily socialize with people because they did the IB. If you met a lot of IB students during your highschool years through various sports competitions then you might be surprised by how many have made the choice to come and study in London.

Would you recommend your university to prospective IB students?

Yes. LCC is consistently ranked amongst the best media and arts universities in Europe – if not the best. If you are looking for a career in media in the city, then a degree at LCC is the way to go. You are in the heart of London and exposed to a multitude of different internships and work placements that you can do in the holidays. LCC encourages its students to think creatively and push their own boundaries.

Further Statistics and Information [University of the Arts, London]

Students		Accommodation	
Undergraduates:	**16,265**	University-provided places:	2,000
Postgraduates:	**1,270**	Percentage catered:	0%
Overseas students:	**10.2%**	Self-catered costs:	£75-£90 a week
Applications per place:	**3.7**		
From state-sector schools:	**97.9%**	**Undergraduate Fees**	
From working-class homes:	**43.7%**	Fees for UK/EU students:	£3,290
		International Student fees:	£9,000-£9,500

London School of Economics and Political Science

Tel. +442079557125; stu.rec@lse.ac.uk; www.lse.ac.uk

Student Name:
D. Cheng

IB World School
Island School, Hong Kong

Nationality:
Chinese

What course do you currently study?
First year. LLB

University offer
38 points. 7,6,6 at Higher Level

How does your workload at university compare to the IB Diploma?

Currently, the workload is around the same. But there is more pressure in other areas, like extra-curricular responsibilities and looking for career opportunities. Different type of studying needed for university. However, a lot of similarities to the IB in terms of time management, essay writing skills etc. I would say it is similar workload.

Would you say you have an advantage over A-Level students in your studies? How?

Yes, because of the multi-disciplinary nature of the IB and the heavier workload, my time management skills are more developed. Also, the independent nature of the IB course meant that I had an easier time adjusting to the independent study required by the LSE. Definitely, a lot of skills I acquired during my IB Diploma years are very helpful when you come to university. I am advantageous since I am used to a lot of workload, so I am more able to finish my work quicker. My essay writing skills that acquired doing History and English are extremely helpful, especially when one is doing law.

Is there any element of the IB that you have found particularly useful in your university studies?

I have found History HL and English HL very helpful to my course, as it trained me in essay writing. Also, the level of information I had to digest and consolidate in those subjects has also allowed me to cope better with the reading required in the law course. Most of my subject revolves around understanding complex principles, reading and writing essays.

Did you find your personal requirements fair? Do you feel the offer under/overrated the IB system?

I feel that the offer under-rated the IB system. In generally, UK universities do underestimate the difficulty of the IB, especially the Higher Level requirements. Getting a 7 in an IB Higher Level subject is statistically a lot more difficult than getting an A* in A-Level.

How does the social life compare to the one you had at school?
The social life is better at university because there are fewer constraints on how you want to spend your time

Are there special efforts made to accommodate international students?
Yes, I had many networking events organized by the LSE and also LSE cultural student societies in my local area during pre-orientation. We even had a pre-departure orientation camp. The LSE also has services and the student union as well as my halls of residence also have international officers in this arena.

Are there many former IB students? Do you socialize with them?
There are quite a few, but of course less than the A-Levels students and yes, the IB students became my closest friends. Most of my friends at my university are actually international, former IB students.

Would you recommend your university to prospective IB students?
Yes, the atmosphere at the LSE is well-suited to former IB students. I would strongly advise everyone to do IB rather than A-level. It is not only increasingly recognised by top-ranking world universities, as one of the most challenging and prestigious Diplomas in finishing high school, but further it expands your mental capabilities by a tenfold. It also provides you with basic life skills, such as effective time management. I feel much more at advantage than all the A-Level students.

Further Statistics and Information

Students		Accommodation	
Undergraduates:	4,200	University-provided places:	3,650
Postgraduates:	4,815	Percentage catered:	36%
Overseas students:	47.5%	Self-catered costs:	£67-£160 a week
Applications per place:	13.8		
From state-sector schools:	70.7%	**Undergraduate Fees**	
From working-class homes:	18.7%	Fees for UK/EU students:	£3,290
		International Student fees:	£13,680

Loughborough University
Tel. +441509223522; admissions@lboro.ac.uk; www.lboro.ac.uk

Student Name:
Rosanna Turner

IB World School:
UNIS, Vietnam

Nationality:
Chilean/American

What course do you currently study?
Second Year. English and Drama

University offer:
37 points.

How does your workload at university compare to the IB Diploma?

I had more work whilst I was at school. Although I have more modules at university than I had subjects at school, there are usually only two assessments per module which are usually no more than 4000 words.

Would you say you have an advantage over A-Level students in your studies? How?

I'd like to believe I do because I feel that I have a more worldly view on many things. I feel I am more open to learning in different ways and I understand the concept of following a criterion. Also lengthy research and writing tasks require less effort.

Is there any element of the IB that you have found particularly useful in your university studies?

The EE was extremely useful in preparing me for university as I know I am able to write a 4000 word essay, and I know the amount of time and work that is necessary for a large research project. ToK I also found very beneficial as it has helped me present my argument in the most effective way possible. The international aspect to the IB has also made me more aware of other cultures and the huge world wide diversity.

Did you find your personal requirements fair? Do you feel the offer under/overrated the IB system?

Personally I feel that the requirements were fair for me, however I struggle to believe that a 6 or 7 in an IB HL subject is the equivalent to a B or C at A-level subject, which many people seem to suggest.

How does the social life compare to the one you had at school?

Extremely different – I am able to go out on a more regular basis and my nights out tend to be a lot cheaper. Loughborough is a pretty small place, not like London, so try not to isolate yourself. There is something to do every night – themed club nights, sport crew dates, events at the student union. You have to keep in mind that Loughborough has a reputation for being a 'sporty' university, and this is in a way true. So if you want to make the most of your social life, you should consider joining a team or club.

Are there special efforts made to accommodate international students?

I am sure there are, however I am not an overseas student albeit my international background. My overseas friends seem to get along fine however.

Are there many former IB students? Do you socialize with them?

There are a couple, and we all seem to get along very well. I don't go out of my way to seek them out though

Would you recommend your university to prospective IB students?

Yes, I suppose I would. Loughborough is a lot of fun for all sorts of students and has so much to offer that anyone who would pass an opportunity to study at Loughborough would be quite silly. I've made great friends and managed to keep a good balance between social life, hobbies, academia and sports. The reputation of the university grows each year in stature and current IB students should definitely check it out as an option.

Further Statistics and Information

Students		Accommodation	
Undergraduates:	11,810	University-provided places:	5,592
Postgraduates:	2,325	Percentage catered:	42%
Overseas students:	9.8%	Self-catered costs:	£2,700-£5,600
Applications per place:	6.9		
From state-sector schools:	22.7	**Undergraduate Fees**	
From working-class homes:	18.7%	Fees for UK/EU students:	£3,290
		International Student fees:	£11,000 - £14,400

University of Manchester

Tel. +441612752077; www.manchester.ac.uk

Student Name:
Lucy Frey

IB World School:
International School of Brussels

Nationality:
American

What course do you currently study?
Graduate, Economics

University offer:
35

How does your workload at university compare to the IB Diploma?

I feel the IB prepared me, as we had to do such a variety of subjects. The workload was more coursework based than my university degree. However, during exam time in Manchester, I was far busier and studied considerably more.

Would you say you have an advantage over A-Level students in your studies? How?

Yes, because we had to be well rounded. By this I mean we had to balance 6 subjects (along with a bunch of other stuff like the Extended Essay, Theory of Knowledge and CAS) and this made us able to handle a lot of different material in a short space of time. A-level students may have gotten more 'depth' from their chosen subjects, but I think overall they do suffer from not having had language, social science, science, and mathematics as compulsory courses.

Is there any element of the IB that you have found particularly useful in your university studies?

Yes I found that Mathematics, Economics, and my Extended Essay gave me a strong basis for my degree. That being said, other subjects such as English and the EE experience gave me a strong writing basis. I was surprised how relevant some of the material covered at a high school level became at university – perhaps this says more about the rigour of the IB program.

Did you find your personal requirements fair? Do you feel the offer under/overrated the IB system?

I feel the IB system was undervalued at the time of applying to Universities, but the year after a direct comparison between the two was offered for Universities to better understand our marks. Strides are being made each year and hopefully in a few years' time we will move past the A-level vs. IB fairness debate.

How does the social life compare to the one you had at school?

I would say they are equally social, excluding the living situation which is far more social due to living with friends. Manchester is a large and vibrant city – always something to do for those who are very social.

Are there special efforts made to accommodate international students?

Yes, there are a variety of societies. Also the university makes sure overseas students are taken care of with regards to fitting in and making travel / luggage storage arrangements during holidays.

Are there many former IB students? Do you socialize with them?

Yes, my two best friends are IB students. IB students are a small minority, but that doesn't really matter. In a few weeks you will really embrace the British university culture.

Would you recommend your university to prospective IB students?

I think it is a great University for socialising. In teaching, a personal relationship with other members of your class and lecturers is highly lacking due the size of the school. Nonetheless, I would not hesitate to recommend Manchester to any current IB students.

Further Statistics and Information

Students		Accommodation	
Undergraduates:	26,070	University-provided places:	9,200
Postgraduates:	6,900	Percentage catered:	30%
Overseas students:	16.5%	Self-catered costs (per week):	£65-£100
Applications per place:	6.2		
From state-sector schools:	78.9%	**Undergraduate Fees**	
From working-class homes:	24.4%	Fees for UK/EU students:	£3,290
		International Student fees:	£11,300 - £14,200

Northumbria University

Tel. +441912437420; www.northumbria.ac.uk

Student Name:
Celine Roels

IB World School:
Antwerp International School

Nationality:
Belgian

What course do you currently study?
Year 1, Fashion Communication

University offer:
TOEFL exam, 6 in HL English

How does your workload at university compare to the IB Diploma?

The workload at university is a more than in the IB. This answer will vary course to course, but overall I would say I have to work a lot harder at university than I did at highschool.

Would you say you have an advantage over A-Level students in your studies? How?

Yes, I feel like I'm able to deal with the workload a lot better, am better in time management and I feel like I have a more overall knowledge then others.

Is there any element of the IB that you have found particularly useful in your university studies?

The Extended Essay and oral exams have definitely helped me out. I am able to hold presentations more easily and I feel like a 2000 word is now nothing compared to all the essays I had to write in the IB.

Did you find your personal requirements fair? Do you feel the offer under/overrated the IB system?

I do think it was fair. I got requirements that I was able to achieve. I wouldn't say easily but there's no point going to a University if you don't have to work for it.

How does the social life compare to the one you had at school?
Social life at University is definitely a lot broader. You make larger groups of friends, and your nights out are not restricted to just a few places. There are always interesting events on, so life never gets boring.

Are there special efforts made to accommodate international students?
Yes. They have open days, then they have fresher's week, where students who are new can meet other students and get to find their way around the area. We also have a Students Union which helps students with any concerns they have. Some overseas students are able to get student loans and are able to earn scholarships.

Are there many former IB students? Do you socialize with them?
I wouldn't say that there are many. But you are able to find several students who have studied in the IB and they are from all over the world, such as Denmark, Germany, Singapore etc. In my flat there are 3 guys that are former IB students. I feel like I am able to socialize with them a lot more than others, as they understand how tough the IB was and how things are so different now from it.

Would you recommend your university to prospective IB students?
Yes I definitely would. It has a variety of courses and everyone interacts with one another. we have so many sport teams that you are bound to find true friends and people you can just chill with. And for my course, I encourage anyone who is interested in the more business side of Fashion to take my course, as it is still very creative but you have the more technical elements to it as well. I haven't had any doubts about my university, location or course and so far it has been an incredible experience.

Further Statistics and Information

Students		Accommodation	
Undergraduates:	17,830	University-provided places:	3,580
Postgraduates:	3,045	Percentage catered:	8%
Overseas students:	11.6%	Self-catered costs (per week):	£68-£105
Applications per place:	4.1		
From state-sector schools:	92.3%	**Undergraduate Fees**	
From working-class homes:	34.0%	Fees for UK/EU students:	£3,290
		International Student fees:	£9,000-10,200

University of Nottingham

Tel. +441159515559; www.nottingham.ac.uk

Student Name:
Laura Astrid Kunas

IB World School:
American International School of Budapest

Nationality:
Canadian

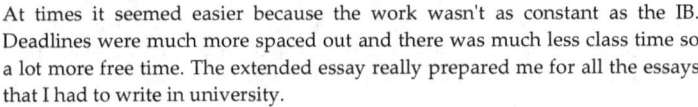

What course do you currently study?
Third year, Art History

University offer:
32 points

How does your workload at university compare to the IB Diploma?

At times it seemed easier because the work wasn't as constant as the IB. Deadlines were much more spaced out and there was much less class time so a lot more free time. The extended essay really prepared me for all the essays that I had to write in university.

Would you say you have an advantage over A-Level students in your studies? How?

Yes because the workload is much greater (more classes) and you learn how to interact with all different types of nationalities. Both of these skills are essential at any university.

Is there any element of the IB that you have found particularly useful in your university studies?

I did art history so obviously art and history were very useful as was the extended essay as mentioned before. Also the teaching was quite similar as they both emphasised the importance of studying on your own. The IB did prepare me rather well to cope with the workload.

Did you find your personal requirements fair? Do you feel the offer under/overrated the IB system?

Yes I think they were fair I was just expecting myself to do much better than I did. I guess it depends on the subject I think with some they're underrated and others overrated.

How does the social life compare to the one you had at school?

It's pretty much the same thing which was good in the sense that I knew what to expect but bad because I'd already experienced 2 years of going out so I got kind of bored of it.

Are there special efforts made to accommodate international students?

Societies were good but I would say on the whole as a university it wasn't that great. Within art history I wasn't treated differently at all. In the case of Nottingham I would also say that before first year they need to stress where the most popular accommodation is so that you can get yourself involved.

Are there many former IB students? Do you socialize with them?

There were 2 from my high school in Budapest and 3 from my high school in Belgium. It was great I loved knowing that I had a friend there that could understand what I was feeling if I needed to talk to someone.

Would you recommend your university to prospective IB students?

Yes because the campus is beautiful, the social life is fun, there are tons of sports/societies to join and it's far away enough from London that you get a true campus experience but if you want to be in the city it's only a 2 hour train ride away. I found that a lot of kids from London came to Nottingham to study.

Further Statistics and Information

Students		Accommodation	
Undergraduates:	21,710	University-provided places:	7,400
Postgraduates:	6,235	Percentage catered:	58%
Overseas students:	15.0%	Self-catered costs (per week):	£107-£174
Applications per place:	6.1		
From state-sector schools:	71.6%	**Undergraduate Fees**	
From working-class homes:	19.1%	Fees for UK/EU students:	£3,290
		International Student fees:	£10,900 - £14,200

University of Oxford
Tel. +44; www.ox.ac.uk

Student Name:
Tim Trueman

IB World School:
King's College School Wimbeldon

Nationality:
British

What course do you currently study?
History; graduate

University offer:
38

How does your workload at university compare to the IB Diploma?

Oxford (and probably Cambridge for that matter) is a very unique place when it comes to amount of 'work' assigned. For most courses, you will find that even though you only have a few tutorial sessions a week (no more than 3 hours of one-on-one or two-on-one sessions), you are assigned a hefty amount of reading and writing to do. Those who are very efficient and escape the temptation to procrastinate will indulge in this type of system because it means you can get the work out of the way early and enjoy the rest of the week without worrying about classes. Personally, I found the first 2 years relatively relaxing compared to the IB because of all the free time. When it comes down to revising for your final exams however, you should expect to study long hours for weeks on end.

Would you say you have an advantage over A-Level students in your studies? How?

As the weeks go by you do start to notice small differences in how A-level students approach their work as oppose to IB students. I do believe that completing the diploma program really does make you an 'investigative thinker'.

Is there any element of the IB that you have found particularly useful in your university studies?

Obviously studying History was essential for my course – and IB History certainly does prepare you for a rigorous graduate degree. Also the fact that I had to keep taking English literature throughout highschool has made my writing and essay structuring skills a step above my peers. The entire experience of the IB is very suitable preparation for the university experience in the UK.

Did you find your personal requirements fair? Do you feel the offer under/overrated the IB system?

If you looked up the percentage of students that obtain a 38+ on their IB diploma and then looked up the percentage that obtain 3 A* at A-Level (the baseline requirements for Oxbridge) I think you would find a wide gap. It is no secret that universities have not yet given the IB program the credit it deserves, but this is improving each year.

How does the social life compare to the one you had at school?
The social life is everything you could want from a university experience. From the Fresher's Week (the first week of partying and socialising organised by the college), to weekly JCR 'bops' (themed parties held at the college) to crew-dates and pub crawls – Oxford really has it all. The students in charge of organising events are always very friendly and there is rarely a day when something 'social' is not happening in college.

Are there special efforts made to accommodate international students?
Certainly. On a university-wide level there are countless societies and clubs that you can join to discover new cultures and nationalities. Individual colleges also do their best to make you feel at home by having 'Overseas Reps' help you settle in and giving storage space to overseas students during the holiday breaks.

Are there many former IB students? Do you socialize with them?
There are a considerable number. You usually discover they did the IB by accident. I've actually met 3 people in my year that obtained a 45.

Would you recommend your university to prospective IB students?
Of course – Oxford is the pinnacle of premium education in the UK. It's a choice that not everyone has and a decision you would never regret.

Further Statistics and Information

Students		Accommodation	
Undergraduates:	11,500	University-provided places:	N/A
Postgraduates:	6,635	Percentage catered:	N/A
Overseas students:	10.7%	Self-catered costs (per week):	N/A
Applications per place:	4.9		
From state-sector schools:	54.7%	**Undergraduate Fees**	
From working-class homes:	11.5%	Fees for UK/EU students:	£3,290
		International Student fees:	£12,200-£14,000

University of Portsmouth
Tel. +442392848484; info.centre@port.ac.uk; www.port.ac.uk

Student Name:
Antonia Stewart

IB World School
Island School, Hong Kong

Nationality:
Antwerp International School

PORTSMOUTH

What course do you currently study?
Year 1, BA Hons Journalism

University offer
31 Points total; 17 at Higher Level

How does your workload at university compare to the IB Diploma?

There are fewer assignments in university but the tasks are much harder and they require a lot of hard work and research. In my opinion, the IB was much easier.

Would you say you have an advantage over A-Level students in your studies? How?

I think A-level students and IB students are equal. I don't really know how the A-level system works.

Is there any element of the IB that you have found particularly useful in your university studies?

I thought the Extended Essay was important especially if attending university afterwards. It gives students the chance to work on time management and practice researching.

Did you find your personal requirements fair? Do you feel the offer under/overrated the IB system?

I think it is quite fair and it does not underrate the IB system. I didn't think that 31 points was too much to ask – given that the IB average is somewhere around 32/33 points. I was very confident of obtaining that total and it was a fair requirement to ask given the nature of the course.

How does the social life compare to the one you had at school?

The social life in university is much different from the social life when I was in highschool as I am now living with other students, I take part in more social events than I usually would and there is so much going on. When you arrive at university you know nobody and this forces you to get out of your comfort zone and become social.

Are there special efforts made to accommodate international students?

I know there are international student societies and there was an orientation for international students at the beginning of the year so they could all meet each other. It's one of those things that you can really get involved with if that's what you're after. Personally, I was more interested in living the typical university life rather than seeking out other overseas students.

Are there many former IB students? Do you socialize with them?

I do not know any IB students from my university yet.

Would you recommend your university to prospective IB students?

Yes. It is a great city with lots of things to do. The university is quite big with so many courses available. The university also offers plenty of activities to join to make friends and be more social.

Further Statistics and Information

Students		Accommodation	
Undergraduates:	15,055	University-provided places:	2,987
Postgraduates:	1,620	Percentage catered:	25%
Overseas students:	9.8%	Self-catered costs:	£74-£117 a week
Applications per place:	4.8		
From state-sector schools:	95.1%	**Undergraduate Fees**	
From working-class homes:	32.4%	Fees for UK/EU students:	£3,290
		International Student fees:	£9,200-£10,500

Queen Mary, University of London

Tel. +448003761800; www.qmul.ac.uk

Student Name:
Faisal Eid

IB World School:
Sagesse High School, Lebanon

Nationality:
Lebanese

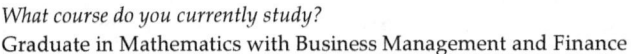

What course do you currently study?
Graduate in Mathematics with Business Management and Finance

University offer:
35 points

How does your workload at university compare to the IB Diploma?

Workload at QM was equivalent to 3/4 or less to that of IB Diploma

Would you say you have an advantage over A-Level students in your studies? How?

Yes in terms of the broadness of materials covered in the totality of an IB diploma. Yet disadvantaged in regards to the amount of work and effort input required to gain entry to top universities, while A level students can concentrate on more specialized and fewer subjects.

Is there any element of the IB that you have found particularly useful in your university studies?

I believe the Internal Assessments required by IB students to hand in such as Lab reports, Economic Article Commentary, World Lit Essays and the Extended Essay all help in preparing students to the professional standards of University assignments and improves students time management skills. Overall, the IB program enables you to get a very good idea of what structure to apply in your essays and coursework.

Did you find your personal requirements fair? Do you feel the offer under/overrated the IB system?

Relatively Fair, yet I still feel the offers provided by universities underrate the IB system. I feel that across the board lower IB score requirements should emulate A-level results.

How does the social life compare to the one you had at school?
I have a much more active social life at university then at school. Firstly the work load is much less and more spaced out , Secondly due to the type of university I was at, unlike most communal campus universities in London, where people come to their classes and leave, at Queen Marys everyone lives inside the university, thus promoting a more social and active student life.

Are there special efforts made to accommodate international students?
Other than priority access to student accommodation I was unaware of any special efforts made by my university.

Are there many former IB students? Do you socialize with them?
I guess there are a significant amount of former IB students at Queen Marys, but I think it plays less of a factor once you start university in forming social circles.

Would you recommend your university to prospective IB students?
Yes I would recommend Queen Marys in terms of its academic strengths and its status as a college of the University of London. The social and university experience is second to none. Due to its area it is also a more economical area to live in, more affordable than central London. That said Queen Mary's is in one of London's most ethnically populated and poorer areas. Where there is little to keep you entertained outside the university gates.

Further Statistics and Information

Students		Accommodation	
Undergraduates:	10,905	University-provided places:	2,257
Postgraduates:	2,010	Percentage catered:	7.7%
Overseas students:	16.4%	Self-catered costs (per week):	£85 upwards
Applications per place:	69		
From state-sector schools:	85.9%	**Undergraduate Fees**	
From working-class homes:	36.4%	Fees for UK/EU students:	£3,290
		International Student fees:	£10,250 - £12,500

University of Reading
Tel. +441183788618/9; www.reading.ac.uk

Student Name:
Alex Schiff

IB World School:
Lincoln Park High, Chicago

Nationality:
Dutch

What course do you currently study?
Second year, Modern History & International Relations

University offer:
6,6,5 in HL subjects.

How does your workload at university compare to the IB Diploma?

Not as many assignments but the essays are more work and more thorough. Coursework consists of essays and sometimes presentations. Presentations are also required to be longer than ones I had to do for the IB.

Would you say you have an advantage over A-Level students in your studies? How?

Yes I would agree with this. I feel I had an advantage in basic essay writing skills. There was a big focus on essay structure and referencing in the first year of university as some students struggled with it I guess. It was not as challenging for me as I had done this in the IB. Then again, A level students have the opportunity to study more specialized subjects than students in the IB which may benefit them in their bachelor and give them an advantage over IB students.

Is there any element of the IB that you have found particularly useful in your university studies?

Higher Level History and the Extended Essay have helped me in terms of preparing for essay writing at university.

Did you find your personal requirements fair? Do you feel the offer under/overrated the IB system?

Yes I do. It is more or less what I expected.

How does the social life compare to the one you had at school?

I go out much more. Many of the student nights tend to be during the week so not many people go out during the weekends. Being in university accommodation in my first year made it easier to settle down and integrate because you live in close quarters with people. Playing a sport is another way to enter the social scene at the university. For example, the hockey team have socials every few weeks

Are there special efforts made to accommodate international students?
In my first year hall of residence there was a representative for international students. There are also various different societies for international students such as the ERASMUS society, international students of Reading University, German society and Italian society.

Are there many former IB students? Do you socialize with them?
I have met only a handful of former IB students. I barely socialize with them as they were not in my hall during first year and so did not see them much.

Would you recommend your university to prospective IB students?
It really depends on what he/she is looking for. The University of Reading is an extremely nice university in terms of its size. It has a nice campus, the sports at the university are well organized and amount of students is not overly huge. Furthermore, Reading is a nice location in terms of travelling. It takes only 30 minutes to get to London by train, and is relatively close to Heathrow airport. However, should he or she be looking for an international environment that somewhat resembles that of international school, I would not recommend University of Reading. Although there are many Erasmus students that come and go throughout the year, there are not many international students doing full 3 year courses. This may make it more difficult for some IB students to settle in and integrate as it always takes time and effort to settle in a different country and culture.

Further Statistics and Information

Students		Accommodation	
Undergraduates:	**9,030**	University-provided places:	4,500
Postgraduates:	**2,315**	Percentage catered:	25%
Overseas students:	**10.8%**	Self-catered costs (per week):	£68.10-£108.7
Applications per place:	**6.5**		
From state-sector schools:	**81.9%**	**Undergraduate Fees**	
From working-class homes:	**26.4%**	Fees for UK/EU students:	£3,290
		International Student fees:	£10,200 - £12,300

Regents Business School (Regents College)

Tel. +44 207 487 7700+44; www.regents.ac.uk

Student Name:
Fernanda Marina

IB World School:
Leysin American School

Nationality:
Columbian

What course do you currently study?
2nd Year – Media Communications

University offer:
Unconditional

How does your workload at university compare to the IB Diploma?

It is quite similar, although IB was a lot of more work. Unlike many other universities in the UK, Regent's requires a fixed attendance rate in order for you to pass the class – and this can sometimes be a hassle. The exams and coursework assignments are pretty simple compared to IB standards.

Would you say you have an advantage over A-Level students in your studies? How?

Yes. IB teaches writing skills that other students do not have, and helps making essays at university easy. At Regents, there are many students who studied their national highschool programs or did the AP program, so it's not just A-Level and IB kids. Nonetheless, you do notice that the kids who studied IB are slightly more prepared to handle the harder work.

Is there any element of the IB that you have found particularly useful in your university studies?

Surprisingly TOK. It helps one to question everything, therefore analysis of literature becomes much more substantial.

Did you find your personal requirements fair? Do you feel the offer under/overrated the IB system?

Yes, the requirements were fair. Regent's is considered a 'private institution' (and this is reflected in their yearly fees). It is not really supported by the government and therefore does not receive the same grants that other universities do. I believe that because of this, they are not too selective in their application process. I would not be surprised to find students who have just passed their IB studying at Regents.

How does the social life compare to the one you had at school?

Both are pretty equal, I chose a school similar to my high school for this reason. At times you forget that you are at university – it is almost like a three year extension of high school. Regent's students are known for their extravagant nightlife parties in London's trendiest hotspots. If you want to experience the finest that the city has to offer, you won't go wrong with Regent's students.

Are there special efforts made to accommodate international students?

Yes. The entire campus feels like a very international place. My four closest friends are all from different countries. There are students from Russia, Germany, Switzerland and literally every country you can imagine.

Are there many former IB students? Do you socialize with them?

There are quite a few, and yes I do socialize with them. Regent's does seem to have a reputation for being the 'go-to' university for children of affluent parents, and many of these students studied at international schools.

Would you recommend your university to prospective IB students?

I would as it's very similar to highschool, however you still get all the independence and fun that you would expect from university. I would say that Regent's is more like American universities then British ones in terms of academia and extra-curricular activities. While it might not have the same reputation that other well-known London universities have, by attending Regent's you are guaranteed an event-filled 3 years and meeting some of the most interesting people. It is a great place for networking and meeting people with a similar drive as you.

Further Statistics and Information

Students		Accommodation	
Undergraduates:	N/A	University-provided places:	N/A
Postgraduates:	N/A	Percentage catered:	N/A
Overseas students:	N/A	Self-catered costs (per week):	N/A
Applications per place:	N/A		
From state-sector schools:	N/A	**Undergraduate Fees**	
From working-class homes:	N/A	Fees for UK/EU students:	N/A
		International Student fees:	N/A

Royal Holloway, University of London
Tel. +44178434455; www.rhul.ac.uk

Student Name:
Olga Evstafyeva

IB World School:
Anglo-American School of Moscow

Nationality:
Russian

What course do you currently study?
Graduate, Mathematics and Economics

University offer:
34

How does your workload at university compare to the IB Diploma?
The workload in terms of hours per week is significantly lower at university, for example I had only about 15 hours a week. However it is necessary to spend a lot of time studying on your own as lectures only give you a 'rough idea' of what you need to know while it is up to every student individually to fill in the gaps. I found that overall I had much more free time than I did during IB, but at the same time the studying was much more focused and I had to be much more efficient when learning. Choosing the right subject was helpful too. Unlike school where you get a mix of all subjects at a very basic level, at university it goes pretty deep into the subject which means you really have to know your basics. If you don't that increases the workload significantly as all of a sudden you find yourself reading high-school textbooks you never thought you'd need again.

Would you say you have an advantage over A-Level students in your studies? How?
I would say that it depends on the set of subjects the other students did. For example in A levels there is Further Maths and Maths, same as IB. But A levels students who did both further maths and maths knew much more than me, even though I did both in IB too. On the other hand I was much better prepared for writing essays and research projects. Also I found that I could find books and other resources better and that my last minute work always looked more polished than that of A-level students, which is a significant advantage in exams. A-level students usually do between 3 and 5 subjects, so I felt like IB gave me an advantage of having practiced almost every type of examination.

Is there any element of the IB that you have found particularly useful in your university studies?
Not any particular element of IB, but I would say the overall experience left me better prepared for my next academic step. University in UK is a completely different type of studying. You have much more time and freedom and it is all up to you to find that perfect time managing balance between social life and studying. That was by far the most difficult aspect of adjusting and unfortunately IB does not prepare for it at all.

Did you find your personal requirements fair? Do you feel the offer under/overrated the IB system?
Yes, I felt the requirements were fair. I remember, before having attended university, that I felt the offer was under-rating the difficulty of IB, but in UK in university you focus on one subject, and in an A-level you cover more topics for the given subject than in an IB HL subject. I found that was the case for me, having done HL maths and further maths I still knew less than those who did A-level maths and further maths, and a lot of my other friends from international schools who did politics, history and etc. Having said that, high school experience is only important first semester of your first year, because after that

everyone is on the same page. So I personally would never choose to redo my high-school and do A level instead because the well-roundness of IB proved to be much more of an asset in the rest 2 and a half years and also gave me much more choice when applying to universities.

How does the social life compare to the one you had at school?
The is much more free time. I would say if you are planning to go to UK, attend all fresher events and join clubs! Most universities don't count 1st year as long as you pass (in Royal Holloway that was the case), which gives you plenty of time to get your time management right and also to have an amazing time so you have no regrets burying yourself in the library for next 2 years.

Are there special efforts made to accommodate international students?
Yes. Firstly I think there was a society for almost every single nationality. Also there is an international student service which helps students to adjust to life in UK. They have a lot of different events for international students too. Furthermore they provide English courses in case you feel like you are struggling understanding the material. Royal Holloway has a lot of international students, so student union and university really try to accommodate every one of them.

Are there many former IB students? Do you socialize with them?
Yes, there were a lot of IB students at my university and yes, I even lived with two former IB students.

Would you recommend your university to prospective IB students?

I would recommend Royal Holloway. I enjoyed every moment there, and after having finished I also went to Imperial for MSc which made me realize how lucky I was to have done mu undergrad at Royal Holloway. It is a true campus university, where the whole town almost solely consists of students. You feel completely safe, and wherever you go you see a friendly face. That also made it much easier to find lecturers because they were always around in case you had a problem. The town itself has everything you need, but as I said it is mostly a students' town, so all events are tied around students union and etc. Also Royal Holloway is only about 30 min away from London by train and 10 minutes away from Heathrow (which is amazing if you are an international student). Furthermore Windsor is only 15 minutes away by car which is a beautiful old town with a lot of things going on, clubbing, shopping, and food. So for me personally it was a perfect combination of studying in a campus university, but with easy access to city life.

Further Statistics and Information

Students		Accommodation	
Undergraduates:	6,590	University-provided places:	2,921
Postgraduates:	1,335	Percentage catered:	37%
Overseas students:	25.8%	Self-catered costs (per week):	£75-£130
Applications per place:	5.1		
From state-sector schools:	78.3%	**Undergraduate Fees**	
From working-class homes:	25.4%	Fees for UK/EU students:	£3,290
		International Student fees:	£11,555 - £13,100

University College London (UCL)
www.ucl.ac.uk

Student Name:
Sana Shah

IB World School:
Oberoi International School (Mumbai)

Nationality:
Indian

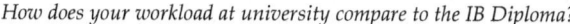

What course do you currently study?
IT with Management, first year

University offer:
34 points, 16 at HL

How does your workload at university compare to the IB Diploma?

Similar as we are loaded with coursework and content wise, large chunks of topics are covered in one lecture whereas in the IB our work (from units) were spread out over several weeks. IB Diploma was work throughout the year, university is work mainly during last 2 weeks of mid- term and of course, exam revision!

Would you say you have an advantage over A-Level students in your studies? How?

To an extent - argumentative skills are more developed through essays (e.g. TOK), EE helps develop research skills and a basic all rounded knowledge before entering university (opens doors for university course choices instead of having to choose after GCSE's/IGCSE's).

Is there any element of the IB that you have found particularly useful in your university studies?

TOK - developing ideas & debating which proposals to choose Sciences (Chemistry & Biology) - learning how to study specifically instead of a whole load of information EE - developing research skills

Did you find your personal requirements fair? Do you feel the offer under/overrated the IB system?

Yes - IB is under-rated as we are loaded with a huge chunk of different content (6 subjects whereas A levels have 3/4) making it harder, yet university offers are fairly similar comparing A level and IB requirements.

How does the social life compare to the one you had at school?
More social life at university as you have more time to manage your social life w/ educational life (in school I had a 8-4 every day, in university I hardly have more than 2 hours or 3 hours a day - plenty of time to finish work and enjoy social life). This is great news for those who are good with time management and don't procrastinate that much.

Are there special efforts made to accommodate international students?
Not really. You do notice that students of a similar background tend to hang out together (the Asian kids with the Asians, the Indian kids with the Indians). UCL is a massive institution so no matter what your personality, you will be able to find someone to get along with easily.

Are there many former IB students? Do you socialize with them?
Not many - I socialize with one who felt similarly about the IB as did I.

Would you recommend your university to prospective IB students?
Yes - even at university it's quite broad, you still have a choice of majoring in a specific area of IT with Management (my course) as it covers the IT aspects as well as management aspects. I am very happy with the academic aspect, and UCL has a very good reputation worldwide. Being based in the heart of London means that you have the world at your feet – whatever you feel like eating, seeing or doing is available.

Further Statistics and Information

Students		Accommodation	
Undergraduates:	11,820	University-provided places:	4,197
Postgraduates:	6,080	Percentage catered:	30%
Overseas students:	29.8%	Self-catered costs (per week):	£91-£165
Applications per place:	9.4		
From state-sector schools:	64.1%	**Undergraduate Fees**	
From working-class homes:	21.1%	Fees for UK/EU students:	£3,290
		International Student fees:	£12,770-£16,725

University of Warwick
Tel. +442476523723; www.warwick.ac.uk

Student Name:
Rishil Mehta

IB World School:
Kodaikanal International School (India)

Nationality:
Indian

What course do you currently study?
Graduated, BSc Accounting and Finance (Warwick)

University offer:
36

How does your workload at university compare to the IB Diploma?

The workload is substantially greater at university than what I had during school.

Would you say you have an advantage over A-Level students in your studies? How?

Big advantage over A-level students due to: - Diversity of subjects in different disciplines - A 4000 essay (extended essay) which prepares you well for assessed university essays - CAS: an activity outside of academics

Is there any element of the IB that you have found particularly useful in your university studies?

Extended essay: its structure and depth prepare you well for university essays - Mathematics and Economics: direct relevance to subject matter - History: greater durability when it comes to writing essays - French: provided a solid foundation from which I achieved fluency in an international language

Did you find your personal requirements fair? Do you feel the offer under/overrated the IB system?

Slightly unfair personal requirement, as I was asked to score a 6 in English, whereas no such condition existed for other exam bodies. IB English had no direct relevance to my undergraduate degree.

How does the social life compare to the one you had at school?
Social life expanded greatly at university as opposed to school, due mainly to the vast numbers of students that made up a truly global atmosphere. - The larger degree of independence also enhanced the social life. Warwick does not have the same type of clubs that you would find in London or other large UK cities, however the events organised by the university clubs and societies are top notch.

Are there special efforts made to accommodate international students?
Many special efforts made: - Orientation at Warwick: a programme that begins 4 days prior to the start of university, strictly for international students, to help them to get better acquainted with life in the UK. - Multicultural students and the vast number of societies - One World Week. I never really felt like a foreigner while at Warwick. There is a large percentage of students from overseas.

Are there many former IB students? Do you socialize with them?
Four in my year and socializing would happen, although not as much as in school

Would you recommend your university to prospective IB students?
Yes I would: - Great reputation with a student-friendly environment - Multicultural atmosphere - Excellent career opportunities afterwards. Warwick's reputation is growing each day. They have wonderful facilities and an excellent business school. From my graduating class, almost everyone now has careers that they enjoy and are proud of.

Further Statistics and Information

Students		Accommodation	
Undergraduates:	11,425	University-provided places:	5,798
Postgraduates:	3,995	Percentage catered:	0%
Overseas students:	18.2%	Self-catered costs (per week):	£75-£120
Applications per place:	8.9		
From state-sector schools:	75.6%	**Undergraduate Fees**	
From working-class homes:	19%	Fees for UK/EU students:	£3,290
		International Student fees:	£11,500-£15,000

University of York
Tel. +441904433539; www.york.ac.uk

Student Name:
Basim Al-Ahmadi

IB World School:
International School of London

Nationality:
British

What course do you currently study?
Politics with International Relations

University offer:
37 points overall

How does your workload at university compare to the IB Diploma?

First year at university was a breeze. IB diploma was more intense over time but at University, I would have very minimal work for 5-7 weeks...but then to meet deadlines in second and third year, at the end of each term, was quite tough. But I would say- pretty equal.

Would you say you have an advantage over A-Level students in your studies? How?

To an extent, yes I do think IB students have a minor advantage over the A-Level students. I feel we can cope better with the pressure of university deadlines, and also we have a more 'worldly' view on topics.

Is there any element of the IB that you have found particularly useful in your university studies?

Yes. In terms of general knowledge and insight- TOK and Extended Essay definitely helped my essay/writing style. I felt also more confident in terms of being international and well-rounded.

Did you find your personal requirements fair? Do you feel the offer under/overrated the IB system?

I think York underrated the IB. To ask me for a 37 and accept A-level students on a AAB is quite unbalanced. Hopefully this will change over the years as the IB program gets better recognition

How does the social life compare to the one you had at school?

It was obviously more diversity- in terms of choosing friends- and I was independent so I can go out whenever I wanted. That flexibility was probably the biggest difference. Yet university at York was quite small- everybody pretty much knew each other- from nights out etc. - so it had a similar feel to the international school I attended.

Are there special efforts made to accommodate international students?

There are a few, yes. Overseas students should not worry with this regard. York makes share to take very good care as the overseas students make up around one-tenth of the overall student body.

Are there many former IB students? Do you socialize with them?

Yes, there were a few but I did not seek them out. I just became good friends with people who shared similar interests as me.

Would you recommend your university to prospective IB students?

Yes I would- 100 per cent. It is not the most multicultural university- but it offers a classic campus university life...something I believe is great to enjoy before entering the real world. My experience here prepared me perfectly for my masters at LSE- both intellectually and socially.

Further Statistics and Information

Students		Accommodation	
Undergraduates:	8,350	University-provided places:	4,540
Postgraduates:	3,145	Percentage catered:	9%
Overseas students:	11.7%	Self-catered costs (per week):	£90
Applications per place:	6.1		
From state-sector schools:	80.2%	**Undergraduate Fees**	
From working-class homes:	21.6%	Fees for UK/EU students:	£3,290
		International Student fees:	£11,300 – £14,850

www.ingramcontent.com/pod-product-compliance
Lightning Source LLC
Chambersburg PA
CBHW070544300426
44113CB00011B/1783